UNLOCKING OCD

Genuine Hope
and Practical Help

By

Nick Buchanan

NLP Master Practitioner (INLPTA)
NLP Trainer (UKAIT)
Dip (Integrative Counselling – Level 5) (UKAIT)
Certificate (Counselling Supervision) (UKAIT)
Dip (Clinical Hypnotherapy) (UKAIT)
BA(Hons). Graphic Design (LJM)
Cert.Ed. (University of Manchester)
Community Life Coaching (Metanoeo / Association for Coaching)

Edited by Stephen A. Hopley

First published 2020

All rights reserved
Copyright Nick Buchanan © 2020

The moral right of the author has been asserted

Nick Buchanan is hereby identified as author of this work in accordance with Section 77 of the Copyright, Design and Patents Act 1988

Book Cover Design by Nick Buchanan © 2020

Book layout and design by Nick Buchanan © 2020

This book is sold subject to the condition that it shall not, by way of trade or otherwise, be lent, re-sold, hired out or otherwise circulated without the author's prior consent in any form of binding or cover other than that in which it is published and without a similar condition including this condition being imposed on the subsequent purchaser

A CIP record of this book is available from the British Library

ISBN   978-1-71679-906-8

Dedication

To all those I have worked with
who have been brave enough
to tackle their OCD
and reclaim the
rich adventure
of living.

UNLOCKING OCD

Genuine Hope
and Practical Help

Special thanks to:

Paul Henderson
Director and Founder of
The United Kingdom Academy of Integrated Therapy
(UKAIT)

Stephen A. Hopley
Who during the course of editing this book
made countless useful suggestions.
This book is richer in every way because of his input.

Disclaimer / Waiver of Liability

The ideas, techniques and approaches in this book have helped *every* client I have ever worked with who suffered from OCD. It is my sincere hope that they will help many others too. If you are a health professional working with clients with autism, schizophrenia or severe psychosis, then you may find that some of these techniques should be modified accordingly or used only with extreme thought and consideration.

It would not be possible to write a book which could suit *every* person with *every* possible condition. However, it would be a shame if I offered no help on the grounds that the help I offer won't work for *every person in every possible mental state.*

If in doubt, please seek advice and guidance from your mental health/health care providers.

I do know from experience that the ideas, exercises and approaches contained herein are suitable and appropriate for the vast majority of OCD sufferers.

I have seen people transformed from hopelessness to hope, from the jail of their own routines to the very adventure of living. With practice, many sufferers can experience the same.

Useful Quotes

'I'm tired of being inside my head. I want to live out here, with you.'
COLLEEN McCARTY (*Mounting the Whale*)

'What saves a person is to take a step. Then another step.'
ANTOINE De SAINT-EXUPÉRY

'The more you try to avoid suffering, the more you suffer because smaller things begin to torture you in proportion to your fear of suffering.'
THOMAS MERTON

'The issue is not that you get symptoms it's what you do with the symptoms that you get.'
FRED PENZEL

'The policy of being too cautious is the greatest risk of all.'
JAWAHARLAL NEHRU

'Our doubts are traitors, and make us lose the good we oft might win, by fearing to attempt.'
WILLIAM SHAKESPEARE (in *Measure for Measure* – Act 1, Scene 4)

'Torture is knowing something makes no sense, but doing it anyways.'
COREY ANN HAYDU (in *OCD Love Story*)

'OCD thoughts are not the problem. Your choice to take them seriously is the problem.'
ANON

'The best way out is always through.'
ROBERT FROST (in *North of Boston* – 9. A Servant to Servants)

Contents

Introduction	17
The Unwanted Guest	20
The Time it takes to OCD	22
What is OCD?	24
Thoughts and Actions	27
OCD is a Liar	31
The Nature of the Beast	34
Not Doing, Doing and Over-Doing	37
Over-Doing Just Creates Problems	41
Resistance is Futile	46
The Thought Displacement Principle	49
Thought Displacement Techniques	56
Objections to Thought Displacers	62
The Critical Moment	65
OCD and Paranoia	67
OCD invokes Fight-or-Flight	69
OCD – The Mind-Parasite	71
Surreal Thoughts	73
What's so good about surrealism?	84
Partners, Friends and Family	88
Bloom's Taxonomy	90
Bloom's Taxonomy and OCD	99
OCD and Responsibility	102
Intensive Thinking	105
You can't argue someone out of their OCD	110
The Left and Right Brain	112
OCD and the Twilight Zone	117
The Future and your powerful imagination	120
The Roots of OCD	123
Using Your Hidden Code	131
Avoiding life itself	135
OCD and Gulliver	137
What do you Really Want?	140
Recovery Summary	153
Key Points Summary	155

Further Information / About the Author
Acknowledgements

**Retire when the work is done;
This is the way of heaven.**

Lao Tzu,
The Tao Te Ching (ninth verse)

Introduction

The ideas and techniques in this book have helped many, many sufferers break free from the chains of their OCD – *for good*. Few people understand the dynamics of this unfortunate condition – indeed many adopt strategies which are shockingly counter-productive.

The circular thought-processes which OCD encourages can only be overcome with a non-linear approach. For example, *trying not to think obsessive thoughts* is a sure way to make your OCD worse. There are alternatives (in this book) which work far better.

Many sufferers are unaware of what is actually happening to them. Some are frightened and most are desperate for answers (which will actually help them to move forwards and away from OCD). This book will give sufferers a much better understanding of their condition, particularly the repetitive thought processes which can be maddening and often debilitating.

My aim is to offer a better understanding of OCD, because once we understand how OCD works, we will be better equipped to deal with it. However, this is not an academic or a scholastic study; rather it is a practical guide with specific techniques which have helped fellow sufferers out of the labyrinth of obsessive thoughts and compulsive behaviours.

> Rule your mind or it will rule you.
>
> Horace

It should be noted that the subtitle to the book is *'Genuine hope and practical help.'* The approach here is a pragmatic one, based on what works and what doesn't work (the latter being just as important).

As a Psychotherapeutic Counsellor, I have worked with many people suffering from OCD. Every one of them found a new way forwards once they used the insights and techniques I am now sharing with you. I wrote this book because I have not found these ideas or techniques elsewhere in any text on OCD. Indeed that's why I originated them. Sometimes if you can't find a tool, you have to fashion one yourself.

The answers you seek won't *happen* to you. This is an immensely practical book. It requires you to *do something different* if you want to get something different. If you make no difference, then there can be no difference. As the great Edward DeBono once said:

You can't dig a new hole
By digging the same hole deeper.

Equally, this is not a book about pain and difficulty. I wish to bring the plaster, not rub the sore. It is about understanding and knowing what works and placing your efforts where (and when) they will have the most effect.

At the time of writing, many celebrities are claiming that they have OCD and they wear their 'infirmity' like a fashion accessory or a badge of honour. They refer to an interest in tidiness or cleanliness as 'my OCD.' We live in an age of victim-chic. The reality of genuine OCD is very different. Those who authentically suffer with OCD would speak of how maddening it is. Most would say it's like being tortured.

It is not something to accessorize with and it makes people limited rather than special.

> People who live with OCD
> drag a mental sea anchor around.
> Obsession is a brake, a source of drag,
> not a badge of creativity, a mark of genius
> or an inconvenient side effect of
> some greater function.
>
> David Adam

The Unwanted Guest

Imagine inviting lots of people to your house for a meal, only to find that long after the meal has ended, one guest won't leave. You ask them politely, but they remain. They stay the night in the spare room. At first you are annoyed, but then you feel so embarrassed about their staying, that you try to hide them from your friends.

Then the unwanted guest starts re-arranging your furniture, your house and your social life. They convince you that it's for your own good and they can even prove that these changes are to keep you safe. So you let them do their thing. But soon they want to re-arrange EVERYTHING in your life. Even so, you find yourself defending the unwanted guest – *'They only want to help me,'* you say. Soon you feel that they are invaluable – you feel that if they weren't there, terrible things might happen to you.

Then the guest spends every day telling you about the dangers and the potential accidents which could befall you. This stops you from living a happy life. You check for potential dangers and this obsessive checking becomes routine. The guest tells you, you must follow the routine. When you check something – *even when you know you have already checked it* – they tell you that you need to check it again... and again. Soon you reach a point where you exist in a permanent state of anxiety bullied by this guest's nagging; in a loop of checking – where you can't get the tormenting voice out of your head.

One day you realize that it is you who are now confined to the spare room whilst the guest has the run of the whole house. Friends and family suggest that you get rid of this unwanted guest because they can see clearly that your life is being ruined. What is really strange is that by this point you feel very strongly that the guest must be defended at all costs – even if it means you falling out with friends or family members. You find that you can use logic very skilfully to justify the guest and their behaviour – even if you are checking things four and five times - because it's best to be thorough. It's best to be safe after all. Who wants an accident? Why court disaster?

Finally, you stop going out. You avoid people. You don't like people criticising your guest. Where possible, you keep your guest a secret; it's your secret and you want less people to know.

Now your life is tailored to the needs of your guest. Your own life has shrunk and diminished and you are now a slave to the life of your guest. You live the way they want you to. You check things, look for dangers and make everything predictable. The guest loves rituals and routines and hates uncertainty and spontaneity. There is less laughter, less social interaction, less risk taking, less love (because love is risky and you could get hurt).

But in time you notice that the guest is never satisfied – they always want more - more rituals and routines. They keep adding to the list of things you should be anxious about.

You feel very defensive when others suggest your guest should leave. You justify them being in your home. But somewhere deep within your core, you know that life could be much better than this. You know that the guest is shrinking your real life, but you are too afraid of the dangers which would befall you if ever you got rid of them. So you carry on... and things get worse.

Then one day you realise fully and without question that the guest has got to go – only, now, you don't know how to get rid of them.

This is the plight of every OCD sufferer I have ever counselled.

The Time it Takes to OCD

How much time do you spend on OCD driven activities? Be as honest as you can (unless of course, you wish to protect the unwanted guest and lie on their behalf?)

OCD Time Calculator	
Hours per day	--
x7 =	Hours per week
x52 =	Hours per year
÷24 =	Days per year lost to OCD

Did you calculate how many days of your life you are wasting in OCD related activities? Most people suffering from OCD are wasting on average 60 days per year in pointless OCD behaviours - that's two months out of every year lost! And if you've been at it for six years then **you've already lost a full year of your life to OCD.** That's 8,736 hours given over to the false pursuit of safety; to the pretend notion that it has all been worthwhile. OCD didn't keep you safe, it merely kept you a slave.

Imagine what you could do with all that time? What have you dreamed of achieving? What would you really *like* to do?

Start reclaiming your time now! Your time *is* your life.

> Security is mostly a superstition. It does not exist in nature... Avoiding danger in the long run is no safer than outright exposure. Life is either a daring adventure or nothing.
>
> Helen Keller

Recovery starts when you are so sick of OCD and realize that you have lost too much of your life to OCD already; when you recognize that you can't continue to live your life this way. That, in fact, it is no life at all and that you want to live differently.

> Habit and routine have an unbelievable power to destroy.
>
> Henri de Lubac

What is OCD?

We all have little routines and rituals. Tennis players bounce the ball a set number of times because they believe it will bring them good luck. I have a habit of shaving the right side of my face before the left. You might always put your left shoe on before your right. Everyone has these habits, rituals and routines. That is only normal. Some habits are useful. They allow us to think about more important things whilst doing routine tasks.

The problems start when these innocent habits become strong addictions; when we *have* to do something, instead of *prefer* to do something. Then, it becomes a compulsion (the 'C' in OCD) not a choice. It interferes with our daily life. Once we are *compelled* to do something, we are no longer a free human being. Our choices are being made for us. We become slaves to our compulsions.

By compulsions we mean ritualized behaviours. The OCD sufferer engages in such behaviours in an attempt to reduce stress, prevent harm or injury. But the stress is usually their own revved up anxiety and the harms and dangers are often exaggerated and imaginary. They do, of course, however, feel real to the sufferer.

When the sufferer's anxiety has grown, they feel compelled to perform a set of mindless physical routines or mental tasks (like counting, naming or repeating) which often replay over and over. These can take up an enormous amount of time and often turn a quick event into a very slow one.

Compulsions are driven by obsessive thoughts (the 'O' in OCD). Such unwanted thoughts, urges and images can be disturbing, intrusive and inappropriate. They often concern themselves with ideas of contamination, symmetry, harm, doubt, religion, sex and health.

With OCD, the sufferer is caught in a trap, frightening and worrying themselves with imagined dangers and silly games. OCD is often about checking, and double checking, and triple checking. Sometimes a sufferer begins their next round of checking when they've only just finished the previous round of checks. Not only is OCD compelling, but it is redundant and useless. It literally serves no purpose. It is meaningless.

> The chief danger in life is that you may take too many precautions.
>
> Alfred Adler

People with OCD will nearly always justify their obsessive and repetitive behaviour with rationalizations. They often become very skilled at this because at the core of all OCD behaviour is a logical premise. For example:

>**Client**: 'It's good to check the electrics are all off before going to bed'
>
>**Therapist**: 'But is it good to check everything *four times* when your first check would do?'
>
>**Client**: 'Well you can never be too thorough, can you?'

This common dialogue pattern reveals a very serious aspect of OCD – the sufferer starts to defend it and shape their lives *to it*. Instead of challenging OCD, they accommodate it and justify it. But the more they give way to OCD, the more it takes over. Soon they will be engaged in covert behaviour; they may, for example, get into work early so that people won't see the way they disinfect their desk and all their equipment.

Feed it and it grows. And it is never satisfied. It wants more!

OCD is a ravenous beast and the more you feed it, the hungrier it gets.

> Don't be afraid your life will end;
> be afraid that it will never begin.
>
> Grace Hansen

Unlike many disorders, OCD must be tackled head on. However there are strategies which give the sufferer ammunition in their battle. The first is, to simply understand how OCD works. When we understand it, we can weaken its hold over us and regain our freedom and human sovereignty. When we have genuine insights about what is happening, we can view the process in a much more empowered way. It is a bit like the old saying 'forewarned is forearmed.'

If you want to tackle it successfully, you must first understand it.

> When the disease is known it is half cured.
>
> Desiderius Erasmus

Thoughts and Actions

With OCD, the link between thoughts and actions has become too strong and too automatic. Every thought is treated as a kind of reality.

The 'O' in OCD is to do with **O**bsessive *Thoughts*

And the 'C' is to do with **C**ompulsive *Actions*

For example consider three different OCD sufferers:

> **John** held his sister's newborn baby for the first time and thought (with caution) *'what if I dropped the baby?'* He then started to think that he must be a horrible person who must somehow like the thought of dropping babies. Inside he feels guilty and ashamed, *'Why did I think about dropping the baby?'* Then his face flushed and he handed the baby back. It was as if everyone else saw his thoughts and knew him to be unsuitable at holding babies. We know, of course, that John's thought was natural and was actually part of his desire *to protect the child and make sure he kept it safe.* Instead he used the thought as if it was a reality and as if he was guilty of a horrible crime. There is often an element of self punishment in OCD. Sufferers feel sometimes that others can read their thoughts.

Of course, the outcome here is that John was unable to share the precious moment of holding a newborn, whilst his sister wondered why he apparently found her child repellent. OCD creates misunderstandings and makes the sufferer increasingly absent from everyday joys.

> **Jenny** would check her car was locked three times before entering her workplace. A set ritual which involved checking the handbrake was on, the doors locked, the windows shut, the wing-mirrors tucked in, the car parked well between the lines of the parking space, etc. But once she was in a meeting at work, a thought would pop into her head *'Did I really check the car properly?'* Once there, the thought *would have to be acted upon.* She couldn't concentrate on the meeting, she couldn't function. *She could only think of the car.* She would always make her apologies and leave the meeting, run out to the car park and check her vehicle *again*. In the end she did this so many times that she was fired from her job. It was her only source of income. Losing her job did not make her reconsider her behaviour. When asked if checking her car so much was getting in the way of her life, she pointed out the dangers of *not* checking her car (*'...if the handbrake's off it could roll into another vehicle...and if I left it unlocked, then it might get stolen, etc.'*).

> **Phil** heard on the news that someone was murdered last Tuesday afternoon in his neighbourhood. He wonders if he could be the murderer *without even knowing*. He thinks back and checks his diary. *Where was he at the time?* He was in work and couldn't have committed the crime. All the same, he asks a colleague to confirm that *he was in work on Tuesday*. Then he worries that he could have slipped out to commit a murder during his break only to return later. He checks again with his colleague that *he was in all afternoon*. Phil's OCD has led him to live in a world where he cannot distinguish between reality and his own private thoughts. Every validation of reality is undermined by his own obsessive thoughts.

In each case there is confusion about what is real and what is not. More specifically there is a blurry boundary between thoughts and reality. The OCD sufferer cannot trust their own memory. Even if they are sure they locked their car – they are still somehow unsure. Just *thinking* about dropping a baby makes them guilty of the *reality* of *actually* dropping a baby, and knowing that a murder has been committed means that they will have to prove their innocence to themselves.

Everyone has unsolicited or uninvited thoughts:

- Was I followed to work?
- Imagine if that cup of tea is poisoned?
- Has someone died because I forgot to switch something off?
- Is my house being burgled?
- What if that stranger on the train platform wanted to push me into an oncoming train?
- Did I kill a cyclist when I drove past them?
- Have I murdered someone and forgot my crime?
- Etc.

Most people simply let such intrusive thoughts go. We all have irrational thoughts at one time or another, but most of us just think of such thoughts as odd or silly. People with OCD, however, hold on to them, giving them serious attention. They treat them as if they were worthy of speculation and consideration – instead of just brushing them aside and moving on to thoughts which are preferable. In this way, *uninvited* thoughts are *invited* in. It is then that they become obsessive and scary. They raise anxiety levels and irrational fears grow and grow.

This, in turn, leads to the sufferer developing habits and compulsions. These are just a way of trying to deal with the anxiety of strong intrusive obsessive thoughts. Most compulsive activities are meaningless and repetitive - lining up shoes, counting things, checking things, etc. But to OCD sufferers they can feel very important; a matter of life or death even! Compulsive activities do lower anxiety levels *slightly*, but relief is only temporary and never complete. There are better ways to deal with obsessive thoughts and compulsive actions, as we shall see.

Left unchecked, OCD will have the sufferer living in a world which is not only very frightening, but also increasingly *unreal*. There's a good reason why this happens. Just take the example of Jenny checking she locked her car. Once she has checked it is locked she gives in to the temptation to check it again. Once she starts double-checking she has entered into a kind of unreality where no amount of checking will suffice. After all, she does the first check knowing that others will follow – so she doesn't do this check properly and mindfully. Then every subsequent check invalidates all the previous ones. In this sense, checking is no longer checking, rather, *it is checking that I am checking* because I am a person who likes checking. It has nothing to do with cars or actually checking them. It is a disorder. It is not healthy or productive.

Checking isn't really checking
-it is checking that I *am* checking.

With OCD, obsessions often curl around issues of contamination, being unsafe or impending catastrophe; these in turn lead to compulsions around cleaning, checking and arranging, which repeat and repeat.

When an OCD sufferer gives in to the desire to check again, they are reinforcing a kind of unreality. They are contradicting their own senses. Our senses are a vital connection with reality – we use them to discern, to understand and to confirm what is actually happening around us.

> My life has been full of terrible misfortunes
> -most of which never happened.
>
> Michel de Montaigne

OCD is a Liar

Some people are pessimistic and they justify their pessimism thus: *I expect the worst and plan for the worst and that way when something good happens it will be a bonus.* What they don't realise is that planning for the worst and expecting the worst often *prevents* any good from happening. Any good that comes along will be missed because they're too busy looking for and expecting a negative outcome.

Imagine wearing dark glasses 24/7 and insisting that there's no brightness in the world.

Life doesn't approach us with things which are all good or all bad. Sometimes opportunities come to us disguised as adversities. On occasions, a difficult problem will carry (at its heart) a gift which will help us. The trick is to always look for the gift. If we don't expect to find it, we will never see it.

OCD is really an *anxiety* disorder. In particular, OCD focuses on risk – the worst that could happen. The *obsessions* and *compulsions* are to guard you against such risks. But the problem is that the risks are both:
   1) Imagined, *and*
   2) Exaggerated out of all proportion

In both of these cases, OCD is indeed a liar. It makes you respond to imagined dangers by getting you to mentally rehearse catastrophes and dreadful outcomes, and in each case the risk is exaggerated out of all proportion.

> When you attempt to eliminate risk from your life, you eliminate along with it, your ability to function.
>
> Fred Penzel

Here's how it usually works:

1) You have an obsessive thought or image (in your mind)
2) You magnify the risk or threat (to yourself)
3) You feel genuine distress and anxiety
4) You are compelled to act a certain way (compulsive behaviour and over compensation)

This is the Cycle of OCD. It is a pattern which sufferers repeat to themselves all day long. In this way, most of their lives are spent in a state of high anxiety and fear.

The sad truth is that *they have been exaggerating risk all along.* They never were in danger. It was just a lie OCD was telling them.

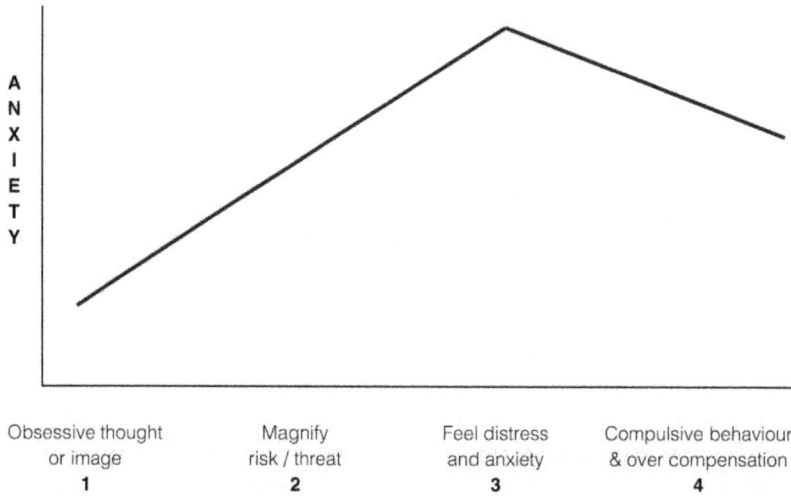

Their compulsive behaviour (stage 4) and over compensation (i.e. over-doing) only alleviates stress *slightly*. They are still more anxious than when they first had the compulsive thought or image pop into their head. But they feel a little better having given in to the compulsion to behave a certain way.

Our fight or flight mechanism is a very useful part of our physiology – it could one day save our lives. But it is only intended for extreme circumstances (life threatening situations) not for petty, imagined ones like - *Did I close the fridge door?*

OCD lies by convincing the sufferer that there is a HUGE danger where in fact there is none. It prepares your whole body for flight or fight – it dumps cortisol and adrenaline in your blood stream, it sends blood away from the major organs to your arms and legs (ready for running or battle). This places a huge stress on the body and the immune system, especially if sustained day in day out.

> No passion so effectively robs the mind of all its powers of acting and reasoning as fear.
>
> Edmund Burke

OCD often wants the sufferer to stay home, because it usually feels like that's the safest place to be. It can be so powerful that it can even make you feel ill if you travel. It has given some people psychosomatic illnesses or made them behave like a hypochondriac.

It doesn't want you to have a life, because real life is risky, so it disrupts work and sabotages relationships. It ruins your social life.

Some OCD sufferers try to avoid situations where they know their anxious OCD thoughts will occur. They will make excuses and give false reasons to others as to why they don't want to: drive the car, leave the house, take the train or call their friend, etc. This makes those around them confused and frustrated. They wonder why the person is acting strangely or irresponsibly. Avoidance doesn't work. It simply grows the OCD. The best way to overcome fears is by doing the thing you fear, not by distorting your life to avoid those things.

The Nature of the Beast

OCD is like a playground bully. If it can torment you, it will. If it can get a rise out of you it will. With bullies, one of the best strategies you can adopt, is *not to change your behaviour to suit them*. Victims of bullying often feel their life shrink to a point of meaninglessness. They can feel trapped, hopeless, helpless and worthless. Sometimes victims modify their lives *to suit the bully* – they might change their route home, alter who their friends are, change how they speak, etc. These all put the bully in charge and once the bully feels in charge – they grow in power and they often want more. Then they dominate their victims *further*.

> OCD is like having a bully stuck inside your head and nobody else can see it.
>
> Krissy McDermott

It is the same with OCD. The sufferer modifies their life to suit what their OCD wants. Soon, OCD is completely in charge, and behaviours become *addictions* rather than *preferences*. And if you think *addiction* is a strong word just remember the words *Obsessive* and *Compulsive* and recall that we are speaking here of a *disorder*. An addiction can be defined easily; it's when we *have to* do something rather than *prefer to* do something.

The following story is relevant to OCD sufferers:

> An old Cherokee was teaching his grandson about life...
>
> "A fight is going on inside me," he said to the boy. "It is a terrible fight and it is between two wolves.
>
> One is evil – he is anger, envy, sorrow, regret, greed, arrogance, self-pity, guilt, resentment, inferiority, lies, false pride, superiority, and ego." He continued,
>
> "The other is good – he is joy, peace, love, hope, serenity, humility, kindness, benevolence, empathy, generosity, truth, compassion, and faith. The same fight is going on inside you – and inside every other person, too."
>
> The grandson thought about it for a minute and then asked his grandfather,
>
> "Which wolf will win?"
> The old Cherokee simply replied,
>
> "The one you feed."

Similarly, our choice is to feed OCD or not feed OCD. We feed it when we entertain *obsessive* thoughts and when we allow ourselves to be *compelled* to act upon those thoughts. When we feed it, it grows, it becomes stronger.

This story carries within it a great truth about OCD, namely that when it is *strong*, then our real life will be *weak*. The space we give OCD *displaces* the space we would normally enjoy in our lives. The more space we give to OCD, the less we will have for ourselves in our lives:

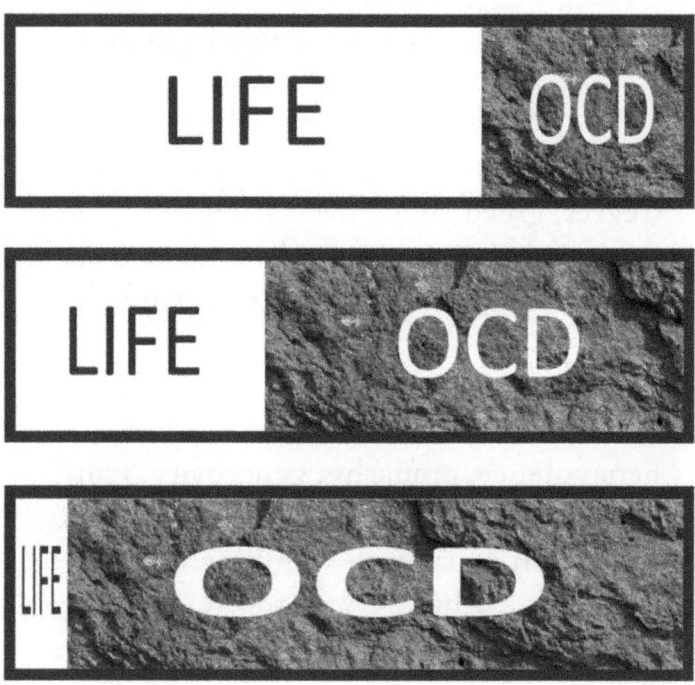

> No amount of security is worth the suffering
> of a mediocre life chained to a routine
> that has killed your dreams.
>
> Maya Mendoza

Not Doing, Doing and Over-Doing

If a thing is worth doing, it is worth doing well. This fair statement is appropriated by OCD sufferers to mean *if a thing is worth doing, it is worth doing again and again and again and again*. And if you were to suggest to them that their behaviour has become counter-productive, they will usually strongly defend it. The problem is that *there is* a logic at the core of their concern, but their compulsive behaviour has become so ritualized and excessive that they are now *a slave to it*. It's as if the robot inside has taken over and their own lives are now less meaningful.

The essence of the problem is this: Whilst *not doing* a task might be neglectful, if we *overdo* a task, then *we might actually be negligent in a different way*. What we want to achieve is *doing* and not *over-doing*. One of the main arguments a sufferer will make is that the task does need *doing*. In the case of washing one's hands or checking one's car is locked, this of course makes sense. However the person with OCD then uses this rationale to justify *over-doing* which simply defeats the object.

It would be negligent not to wash one's hands or to leave one's car unlocked. Obviously 'Not Doing' is not advisable.

Not Doing > Doing > Over-Doing

The healthy position is to move from *Not doing* to *Doing*. But the OCD sufferer moves from *Not Doing* directly to *Over-Doing*. They behave as if mere *Doing* doesn't exist.

Over-doing is the domain of OCD. The problem with over-doing is that it is done mindlessly – quite literally *on auto-pilot.* For example, a sufferer checking that their car is locked after parking, will do the first round of checks. But they won't do these first checks properly, because they know they will double and triple check it. So each check is done *without it really meaning anything.* The first check doesn't count (because they know that other checks will follow), and then every subsequent check is followed by another and another – each check *invalidating* all previous checks.

Over-doing is *the opposite* of doing.

The following chart will give us a richer understanding of the exact nature of OCD's *over-doing.* The bullet points underneath the chart will explore the particular dynamics of each row:

NOT DOING	DOING	OVER-DOING
Neglectful	Healthy	OCD
Irresponsible	Responsible	Irresponsible
Inattentive	Attentive	Inattentive
Out of Mind	Mindful	Trance (Out of Mind)
Task not done	Task done	Task not done
Creates Problems	No Problem	Creates Problems
Child Mode	Adult Mode	Child Mode
Not Functioning	Fully Functioning	Not Functioning
Need to do More	Just right	Need to do Less
Not Checking	Checking	Not Checking (you're checking that you're checking)

Starting with the first row which admits that *'Not Doing'* would be *'neglectful':*

- Clearly if we don't do something that needs doing, we are being **neglectful**. So when we do it, it is a **healthier** situation. But then if we overdo it, then we place ourselves in the realm of **OCD** (driven by our obsessive compulsions).

- Not doing something which needs to be done might be considered **irresponsible**, so we do it and act **responsibly**, but then if we overdo it we become **irresponsible** because what we are doing is no longer what needs to be done.

- If we don't do something which needs to be done, we might be **inattentive** – our mind might be elsewhere – but once we attend to the task in hand then we are being **attentive**. If however we overdo the task, then we become **inattentive** once more. We are stuck in an endless routine rather than completing and attending to a finite task.

- If we put something **out of our mind** and avoid a necessary task then the task goes undone. Once we choose to do the task, then we become **mindful** (we consciously get the thing done and notice when it is complete). When we overdo a task then our routine and robotic program puts us in a kind of **trance** – we are in a sense absent, out of our own minds.

- If we don't do, then the **task remains not done**. When we do, then the **task is done**. When we overdo, however, there is a sense that the **task is not done** (again), because no amount of checks and balances will suffice. We never feel satisfied that it is done - we always need one more check, one more wash of the hands, or endless proof that we didn't unknowingly run over someone on our way to work.

- Leaving things undone **creates problems**. Getting the job done means there is now **no problem**. But if we overdo then we are **creating problems** because we no longer trust our own eyes – we regard our senses as unreliable. This is a huge problem.

- When we avoid a task, then we could be said to be in **child mode** – we are not functioning as a responsible adult. Once we face the task and get it done we are in **adult mode**. But if we stay with the task, never completing it, unsure if it is done enough then we are no longer functioning as an adult (who can make decisions and stick by them) but rather we have returned to **child mode**.

- In the same way we are **not functioning** well when we need to do a task and haven't yet done it. Once we do it, we could be said to be **fully functioning** in relation to that task. But if we overdo it, then of course we are **not functioning** properly because our efforts far exceed the outcome. Neither are we being efficient with our energy because with OCD we can never know when enough is enough.

- If we haven't done something, then we **need to do more**. When we do it, it is **just right.** When we overdo it then we should be **doing less** – often *far less than we are doing.*

- OCD sufferers often like to check things. **Not checking** is their greatest fear. **Checking** can be sensible and useful -but when we over-check then what happens is that instead of actually checking something and confirming that it has been done, the over-checking becomes the same as **not checking** because it doesn't actually satisfy the sufferer (who needs to check and check and check again). In the end of course they are not checking what they think they are checking they are just checking that they've checked.

So you will see that over doing *has nothing in common with doing*. Furthermore:

Overdoing isn't the same as Doing something well.

And:

Overdoing is just another way Of Not Doing.

I have laboured this point because it is very useful for the OCD sufferer to understand that when they overdo things, they create problems for themselves and for the things they are dealing with.

Over-Doing Just Creates Problems

Even outside of the realm of OCD, *over-doing* things can have dramatic effects. Here are three short examples:

1. My father in law was a very good and kind man and he liked to do DIY jobs together. His last five years were blighted with Alzheimer's disease but he still enjoyed basic DIY tasks. One day I invited him to help me file off some rust from my front gate in preparation for priming and painting. There was a flat scroll of decorative metal at the top of the gate which had a few rust blisters. It was a simple task and he liked to feel involved and helpful. We worked together on different parts. Because of his Alzheimer's, my father in law had lost the *meaning* of what we were doing. At one point I had to take a phone call. When I returned, he had filed not only the rust off, but right through the metal. The top decorative scroll was ruined.

This is how it is when we *overdo* things – it isn't better – it's worse! Of course, it wasn't my father in law's fault and I expressed no disappointment. That would have been unfair. He was doing the best he could. I simply told him he was doing a great job – and then I diverted the task to sawing off the top scroll entirely and smoothing a flat top to the gate. Our gate is now missing its decorative scroll. Since Joe's passing, his family are now all missing a beautiful human being. Gates can be replaced. What was important that day was that Joe was happy, and felt wanted and valued – which he was – and that we shared the warmth of our friendship.

2. There is a well-known child's game where you take a common word – *e.g. elbow* – and say it out loud 50 times. The more it is repeated, the more abstract the word becomes. Eventually it is no longer the familiar word you might use, it becomes instead a meaningless sound – a strange thing. In the case of *elbow*, you might even notice that you form the word by bringing the tip of your tongue to the back of your front teeth and then after closing your mouth you create a pressure of air then as you expel it, you make your mouth into a tight circle. How strange it all is. One important thing to notice is that (due to its concentrated repetition) the word's meaning evaporates and all we are left with is a strange sound in the mouth. *Overdoing* tends to reduce meaning.

3. I knew a man who was **an industrial plumber** working at huge petrochemical plants. He worked with giant nuts and bolts - huge great clunky things – bigger than a hand-span. He seemed to get laid off regularly and, because he took it so personally when he did, I discretely asked his friends if they knew the reason. They said that he had a habit of over-tightening the nuts and bolts. It turned out that he would tighten the nut on the bolt, *but then would give it another turn just to be sure…then another just to double check…* (and remember these long industrial spanners had tremendous leverage and torque) … *then he would tighten a little bit more…* and then the heavy nut would sheer off the bolt end completely and drop with it to the floor. He did this regularly, and even though he could see that it was counter-productive, he couldn't stop himself from 'double-checking.' To him, *a loose bolt* was a problem. He didn't appreciate that *a sheered off bolt* was a much worse problem - *because it couldn't be fixed.*

Over-doing creates problems. The problems it creates are either equal to the level of problems caused by *not doing* something – or *even greater* (after all a sheered off bolt can't be fixed but a loose bolt can be tightened).

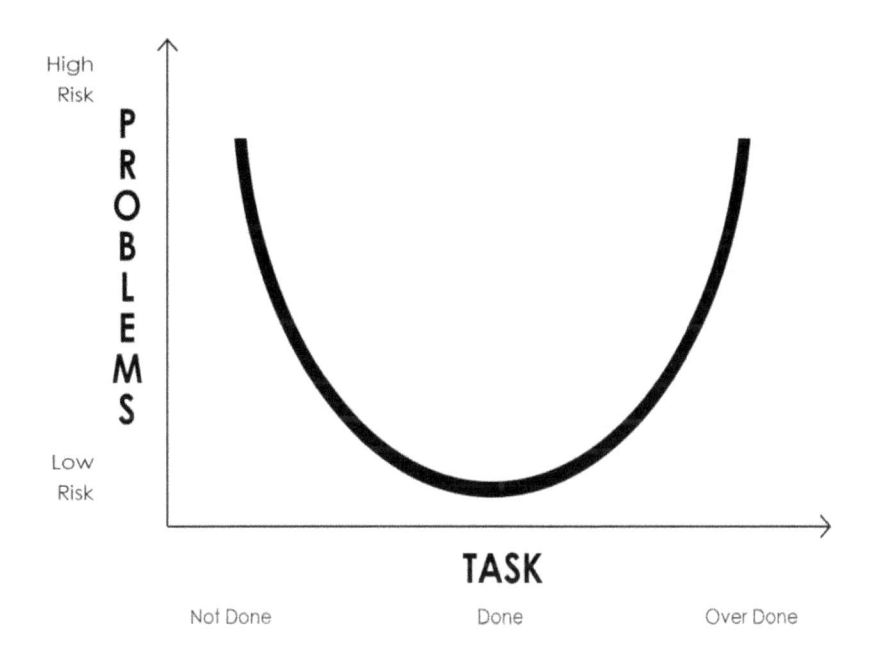

PROBLEMS (High Risk to Low Risk) vs **TASK** (Not Done / Done / Over Done) — U-shaped curve.

As long as a person with OCD reassures themselves that what they are doing is simply *a thorough job*, then they will see no reason to change. Furthermore they will be feeding the insatiable monster – Obsessive Compulsive Disorder. It is only when a person recognises that *over-doing* is not the same as *doing something well*, that they can begin to oppose such behaviours. This is an important step which makes progress more likely.

We can all fall victim to *over-doing*. I recently went to a concert performance of Mahler's 5th Symphony by the Liverpool Philharmonic Orchestra. Before the start I turned off my phone. I would be mortified to receive a call in the middle of a quiet passage! A little later, just before the first notes were played, I felt *a strong urge* to double check that my phone *was indeed* off. But I stopped myself because *I knew that I had checked it*. It was, of course, off. Had I given in to the impulse to check again, then I would be putting myself in the loop of checking and double-checking – all of which would be *over-doing*.

If you use a razor to shave and you ignore the fact that you have completed your shave (having successfully shaved away the unwanted hair / stubble) then you will keep on shaving and the over-shaving will give your skin a very nasty shaving rash - eventually you will start to bleed. Shaving is fine, but *over-shaving* is not.

When you apply your handbrake it works fine, but if you have a habit of *over-pulling* it then it will quickly become slack and may even become ineffective.

Over-doing creates its own dangers. It is much safer to simply do, and move on.

The real gains for the OCD sufferer are made at precisely this moment – just when the urge to re-check or re-do something is strongly felt.

The re-checking urge must be avoided. If you give in to it, then you will be reinforcing behaviours which will have you stuck in a mindless loop.

It is vital that OCD sufferers learn to notice when doing has drifted into over-doing. This boundary is deliberately blurred with OCD. It will try to convince you that you're just doing (and not over-doing). If you can re-establish the boundary between doing and over-doing you will be taking a very important step. Then you will be better placed to stop once something is done, and move on and not check it again.

There are many strategies, approaches and tips which will help you to overcome your OCD and the ones which I have found to work best are all in the pages of this book.

> Some things we check,
> and double check, and lose.
>
> Prefab Sprout ('Horsin' Around')

Overdoing is a habit and like all habits it feels comfortable, it is familiar. It gives us comfort. When we learn to just *do* – and not *overdo,* it will feel uncomfortable at first – it may even feel *wrong*. But you must be committed to it as an outcome if you are to overcome your OCD. When I say 'committed,' I recognize that it may take some time and practice to stop once a thing is done and not persist in overdoing. But you must be committed to this new practice of walking away and refusing to overdo once something is done. *If you want your life back, this is where you must place your efforts.*

It is only when an OCD sufferer recognises that *over-doing* is not the same as *doing something well*, that they can begin to oppose such behaviours.

> *To keep on filling*
> *Is not as good as stopping.*
> *Overfilled, the cupped hands drip,*
> *Better to stop pouring.*
>
> *Sharpen a blade too much*
> *And its edge will soon be lost.*
> *Fill your house with jade and gold*
> *And it brings insecurity.*
>
> *Puff yourself with honour and pride*
> *And no one can save you from a fall.*
>
> *Retire when the work is done;*
> *This is the way of heaven.*
>
> *Tao Te Ching by Lao Tzu.* (ninth verse)

Resistance is Futile

Despite the title, this chapter contains hope, through a secret truth which few have found:

> That which you resist, persists.
>
> Anon

When we resist something, we are actively pushing it away. It becomes the object of our attention. We home in on the very thing that we don't want, and we use all our energy concentrating on it and pushing it away. But if we are busy pushing something away, we are always *connected* to it. It is only when we let go, and give our attention to something else that we can truly be free.

Remember, whatever we give our attention to will become more real for us.

Trying *not* to think of something is a waste of time. Try not to think of a beach ball. I bet you just thought of a beach ball! But this is precisely the double-bind that many OCD sufferers get themselves into - and they do it with the best intentions. They think thoughts like these:

*"I don't want to think **about checking the car is locked again**"*

*"I'm going to resist **my OCD behaviour** this time"*

*"Okay here we go. I'm **not** going to check **the plugs are all switched off again**."*

*"I will forget about **the car** entirely"*

*"I'll try not to think about **the light switches** now that I have come to bed"*

All of these responses are self-defeating because they make their focus the very thing they are trying to avoid. *Resisting a thought only strengthens it.*

Incidentally, people do this in other ways every day. They say things like *"Don't **forget the meeting** on Tuesday"* when those who have studied NLP would know that more people will memorize the appointment if instead you say *"Remember the meeting on Tuesday."*

It is about directing your attention towards *what you want*, not *what you don't want*. It does not make sense to go shopping with a long list of things you don't want. It may leave no room for what you *do* want.

A parent whose child is carrying a very full glass of milk into the living room would be unwise to say, *"Don't **spill the milk!"*** The focus of which is obvious. It would be far better to say *"Well done, **you have a steady hand. I bet you can keep all of the milk in the glass.**"*

Sometimes signs are placed in public places like train stations and bus depots, worded like this:

Shopping List

I don't need
- Bread
- Milk
- Peas
- Apples
- Oranges
- Pizza
- Olive Oil
- Green Peppers
- Onions
- Tissues
- Deodorant
- Toothpaste
- Shampoo

> **WE DO NOT TOLERATE ABUSIVE OR AGGRESSIVE BEHAVIOUR**

This nearly always lead to a rise in such behaviour. Better signs might be worded something like this:

> **Thank you for being courteous and polite. We value your custom, and we will behave with courtesy towards you.**

So remember: *resistance is futile because it drives you towards the very thing you wish to escape.* Why focus on what you don't want? The good news is that *resistance is unnecessary.*

As we shall see in the next chapter, the secret is **that you don't have to resist.** Obviously you don't just do nothing. There are many things you can do - which work – one of which I call **Displacement**.

The Thought Displacement Principle

Imagine feeling very calm and relaxed *whilst at the same time feeling* furiously angry. It is not possible. You cannot experience two very different emotions simultaneously. They are mutually exclusive. Indeed Shakespeare said the same when he paired opposing emotions and said that no man could experience them both at once:

> Who can be wise, amazed – temperate, and furious,
> Loyal and neutral, in a moment? No man.
>
> William Shakespeare (*Macbeth*, Act 2, Scene 3)

As we begin to relax, our brain cycles drop first into what is known as the *Alpha* state (8-13cps) and then deeper into *Theta* (4-8cps) and finally deeper still into the *Delta* state. It is not possible for our brains to operate low and high cycles simultaneously. When we are very anxious, we are in the high end of a state known as *Beta* which is represented by much quicker cycles (14-30cps).

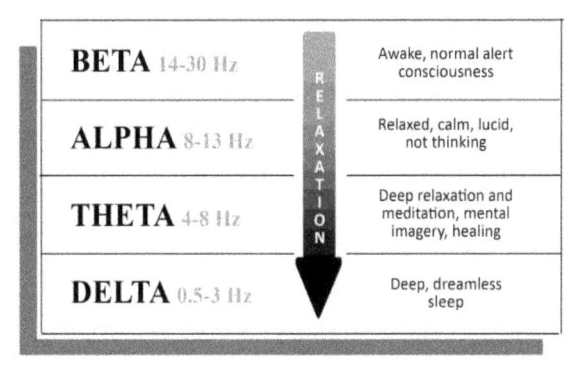

BETA 14-30 Hz	R E L A X A T I O N	Awake, normal alert consciousness
ALPHA 8-13 Hz		Relaxed, calm, lucid, not thinking
THETA 4-8 Hz		Deep relaxation and meditation, mental imagery, healing
DELTA 0.5-3 Hz		Deep, dreamless sleep

As a Clinical Hypnotherapist I have witnessed the tremendous solace that can be gained from relaxing the body. Because mind and body go together, a relaxed body will be a balm to an anxious mind. Equally, if the mind remains too busy, then it will be difficult for the body to find repose. The mind-body connection is very strong - ask any psoriasis sufferer what happens to their skin when they are very anxious.

When an emotion is experienced strongly, it tends to displace all opposing or dissimilar emotions.

This concept of *displacement* is a very useful one. As we shall see, it can help us devise powerful strategies which can give the OCD sufferer tremendous gains.

Not only can *emotions* displace other *emotions* – but *thoughts* can displace other *thoughts*.

> Take a moment to visualize (very clearly) a small friendly baby elephant – *really imagine it. See it in your mind's eye* (close your eyes if it helps):
>
> Picture its wrinkly grey skin and its large flat ears.
> Smell the scent of its bedding.
> Notice the way it moves slowly.
> Observe its loose skin and its baggy-pants walk.
> Feel the textured surface of its skin.
> See those large cylindrical feet.
> Notice its trunk and the way it sniffs things to explore.
> Its wet nostrils quiver.
> It has bristly eye-lashes and a stringy tail.
> Make the elephant as real in your mind's eye as you possibly can.

Now try this:

- Don't think about that **grey elephant**.

- Stop thinking about that **baby elephant the one with the large flat ears.**
- Try not to **picture the elephant** or its trunk or its feet.

Obviously from the previous chapter, you will be aware that when someone asks you *NOT* to think about an elephant – it makes you think about an elephant. It doesn't work. If you stopped a random person on the street and asked them *not* to think of a guitar – guess what they would think of? The answer may be obvious, but the principle is, nevertheless, profound. So let's now build a technique out of this fact which will help you escape from obsessive thoughts – *if you practise the technique.*

Trying not to think of something is a waste of time. This is one reason it is useless to tell someone NOT to worry. It *harms* exactly where it seeks to *heal*. So it is useless telling an OCD sufferer *not to check* the light switches again. It is just as useless (if you are an OCD sufferer) to *try not to do* what OCD wants you to do. In a moment we will examine what really does help, but before we do, there is something else we must do.

I don't know if you are familiar with Amazonian tree-frogs? Some are a bright acid-green colour with large suckers on their feet. They can leap from tree to tree, landing on large flat leaves. They look wet and waxy. You may have seen some of them on nature programmes. Do you know the ones I mean? They have large bug eyes protruding from the tops of their heads and their bright green bodies are covered with slime. Some inflate their necks like balloons to create a calling sound to attract a mate. Have you seen them – or seen similar frogs?

Did you notice that while you were picturing the tree frog, all thoughts of elephants were gone from your mind?

This principle is more profound than most people realize. Take a moment to realize that **you just controlled your thoughts and chose which ones to think.** You made the elephant thoughts disappear and replaced them completely with thoughts of a tree frog. **It really is possible to take charge of your thinking.**

At this point it is worth remembering that thoughts are only thoughts, they are not *you. You are much more.*

We all have thousands of thoughts every day. Some are weird, scary or negative. We all have such thoughts. *Everyone does!* We are not responsible for the thoughts which come into our heads, but *we are responsible* for those we *choose to take hold of* – those we *feed and focus on.* As the great Zen master, Shunryu Suzuki, said:

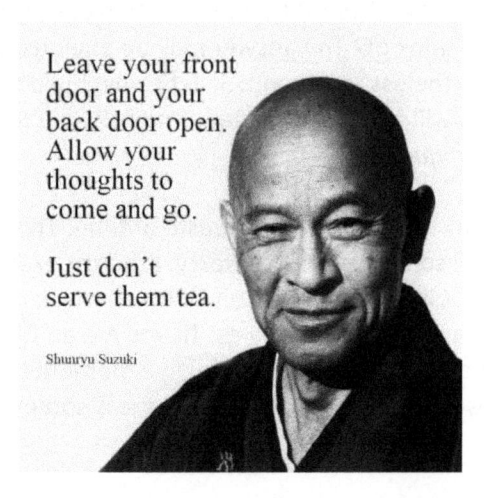

> Leave your front door and your back door open. Allow your thoughts to come and go.
>
> Just don't serve them tea.
>
> Shunryu Suzuki

This is because:

Whatever you give your attention to will become more real for you.

A weird or negative thought is not the problem. The problem is the over-reaction to the thought. That's what gives it energy and puts you on high alert. What you focus on, grows. It is that simple. *Attention is a choice.* What thoughts will you be growing? Which ones are you going to feed and nurture? So you will understand that a weird, scary or negative thought is not the problem. The problem is when you overreact to those thoughts and hold on to them. That is what gives the unwanted thoughts energy and it is that which puts you in a state of fight or flight.

The big lie of OCD is that you have no control, and since taking control will feel uncomfortable (at first) people often give up too easily and the lie continues. But OCD is only a habit. Let that sink in for a moment. It is just a way of doing things that we have repeated and got used to. Eventually, we operate from a kind of auto-pilot, believing that *it has to be this way* – as if the other choices were somehow unavailable to us. As if it has become part of who we are.

> We first make our habits, then our habits make us.
>
> John Dryden

But there is hope, because:

> "Habit is overcome by habit."
>
> Thomas à Kempis, c. 1420

In a moment, I want you to put this book down and try something. I want you to simply fold your arms – just the way that you usually fold them without thinking. Once folded, you will notice that one of your hands *tucks in* downwards whilst the other *pops up* with its fingers pointing upwards - notice which of your hands does which.

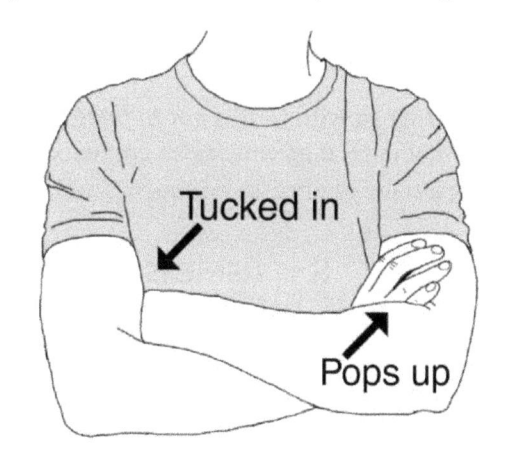

Now I want you to fold your arms again *but this time do it the other way around so that the hand that tucked in, now pops up (and vice versa).* In other words fold your arms 'the other way.' Give it a try.

Before you read on, make sure that you have done the exercise. ***It is important that you experience the difference.***
Okay. Now what I want you to notice most of all is *how it felt*. How

was it for you? Often new things feel funny, odd or wrong. This is because they are not our usual way of doing things. In folding your arms the 'other' way, you were no longer on 'auto-pilot' – no longer simply allowing habit to set your default. Even though this alternative way of folding your arms feels 'wrong' – it is of course precisely how thousands of other people fold *their* arms – and to them, *your way feels wrong.*

You just disabled your *auto-pilot* and *flew solo.* Normally when we fold our arms, we do it automatically – and we do it the *same way every time*. This is a useful habit because it means we don't have to think about it every time we fold our arms. And of course it is of no consequence which way we fold our arms. So we could regard our auto-pilot here as a *good habit, a helpful habit.* After all you don't want to think about which way to fold your arms *every* time you fold them.

But what about *bad habits?* What about things we have learned to do *automatically* which, even though they harm us, still feel comfortable to us? OCD is a bad habit which has been so reinforced with use that it now feels comfortable. It might feel 'natural' or 'normal,' even though it is malignant and an imposter.

The challenge with OCD is *not to fight the OCD*, but to *replace it* with other habits. Habits which give you your life back and which stop you being a slave to obsessive thoughts and compulsive behaviours.

It is useless to *try not to do* what OCD wants you to do.

The displacement techniques which follow will require effort and commitment. We should remember that when we try things which are not our usual way of doing things, *we will often feel uncomfortable*. As we have said, it may even feel *wrong*. But with practise, the unhabitual will eventually become habitual. If you practised folding your arms the 'wrong way' every day, it would no longer feel weird. What once felt wrong, could soon feel right.

New habits can be learned. The bad habits of OCD can be overcome by the good habits we choose. ***Thought displacement*** is one of those good habits. OCD sufferers I have worked with have tried it and found it to be *very* effective, especially *if it is practised* until it becomes a habit.

> There are some things one can only achieve by a deliberate leap in the opposite direction.
>
> Franz Kafka

The next chapter shows you how you can use the Thought Displacement Principle with some specific techniques.

Thought Displacement Techniques

The principal behind these techniques is deceptively simple yet incredibly powerful. The thought of an elephant can be dissolved completely when we visualize something else entirely (e.g. a tree frog).

An OCD thought – even a persistent and obsessive one - can be neutralized (with practice) with a completely different thought, *if* it is absorbing and compelling enough.

First, you have to *want* to change. It is useful to focus on all the reasons you no longer want to entertain your OCD. Think of how it has been adversely affecting your life. Picture the life you would prefer.

The secret is to flood your mind with engaging thoughts about something completely unrelated; it could be **something complicated** which requires your full attention, or **something you love to think about** and into which all your thoughts can happily tumble. Here are some examples which have proved useful with my clients. You might like to try one, some or all of the following. Not all will appeal to you. *Find the ones that appeal to you most and use them.* You will find that this strategy has tremendous power to displace the thoughts and feelings you don't want – *if* you use it fully. Like all skills, this takes practice. It might feel uncomfortable at first but if you stick with it, you are likely to make huge gains. Here are some very practical ways in which you can displace unwanted obsessive thoughts:

A: *Plan a holiday just in your mind* (i.e. without using pen and paper) work out where you would like to go; list as many destinations which might appeal to you. What types of different holidays do you like? Work out how much it will cost. Who you will go with? When you would choose to start saving. What will you choose to pack? Rate your previous holidays out of ten. Recall as much as you possibly can about each of your previous holidays (places, people, events). Etc.

B: *Christmas gifts* – consider each friend and family member in turn and work out which gifts would make an ideal present for them. Hold each person in your attention in turn. Be specific – think about their likes and passions. Come up with as many gift ideas as you can for each person.

C: *Do a complex maths problem* – in your head. Recite your nine times table or your thirteen times table (go beyond the numbers you usually stop at), divide 22 by 7. Multiply two, two-digit numbers (e.g. 27x14).

D: *Contemplate a paradox deeply* – consider its meaning and really explore its contradiction. Contemplate it with all your attention. Here are some examples:

- What would it *mean* if you saw a sign which read 'This is not a sign?'
- What if you bought some powdered water, what would it be like and what would you add?
- If you type the letter A, then delete it and re-type it, is it the same letter?
- What about a sign which says "Please ignore this sign." Can it be observed and obeyed?
- If a flag has holes in it, do they flap in the wind too?
- Can we think the unthinkable?
- If God is all powerful, could she build a wall too high for herself to jump over?
- Banks lend you money only if you can prove you don't need it.

- Isn't it amazing that cats have two holes in their coats exactly where their eyes are?
- Youth is wasted on the young.
- When you listen to music, do you *hear* the spaces between the notes?
- Art is a lie which makes us realise the truth - Picasso.
- Imagine a country where those condemned to die are allowed to decide whether they will be hanged or beheaded by making a statement. If their statement proves false then they will be hanged; and if it proves true then they will be beheaded. A condemned man, when asked for his statement, says cleverly, "I shall be hanged."

The nature of the paradox is not important.

The main thing is that you are able to engage your mind in a new direction.

Never take the paradox on face value, but rather consider its implications and explore the different ways the problem can be approached.

E: *Musical calculations* – if you are familiar with musical notation, you might like to do some calculations in your head. For example you might take each major chord in turn and work out its relative minor (for example the relative minor of A Major is F#minor, the relative minor of F Major is D minor, etc.) Or you might consider a song for which you know the chords and try transposing the song five semitones higher (so B7 becomes E7, A minor becomes D minor, etc.). This is taxing for most non-professional musicians.

F: *Joke writing* – try to write a joke from scratch. Because this is taxing and complicated, it demands your full attention. Think of a profession or a situation (a doctor's waiting room, a teacher in a school, two tramps on a park bench, a football player, etc.). There might be a dialogue.

What is the punch-line? Craft it until it works as well as it possibly can. Then write another about a totally different situation. This is very taxing and difficult – and that is part of its use.

G: *Plan a 'vision-board'* – of images which express your goals in life. What sort of pictures would sum up each goal? Where will you find such pictures? Are there any phrases or quotes which you would wish to be included on your 'vision-board'? How would you arrange the images and words? Will any images take priority? Will a narrative emerge in any sequence of images? Are some related?

H: *Consider the next five years of your life* – what changes would you like to make? It may help if you think about each of the following areas in turn: Health and fitness; Relationships; Finance; Self Development; Helping others; Dreams for the future; etc.

I: *Write a poem* – start it just in your mind, then when you have a few words, commit it to paper and try to find the next line, and the next. You might consider a wide range of subject matter. Your poem might be about something you can see, or once saw, a place or a thing, or it could be about a feeling. You might use comparisons (metaphors and similes) to express the nature of the thing you are describing. What is it like? It could be serious or funny or just interesting.

J: *Compose a limerick* – just start a line with a placename at the end and see if you can write the next four lines (e.g. *'There was an old man from Stroud,'* or *'There once was a woman from Ditton,'* or *'There was a young girl from West Ham,'* etc.). Like the previous thought displacers, this exercise is useful because it absorbs your attention, but it also carries with it an added bonus – the results are often funny and humour is the biggest enemy of the robot mind.

Fun is the enemy of OCD - and humour challenges categories.

The form of a limerick is this:

> *There was an old man from Leeds*
> *Who bought a packet of seeds*
> *He sowed them for hours*
> *And thought they were flowers*
> *Now he's digging them up on his knees*

It doesn't have to be hilarious (as you can see) but it should be well crafted and worked at.

Etc: *Invent your own thought displacer* – you might come up with a new thought displacer which works great for you – so long as it is thoroughly absorbing, distracting, and engaging. Something which demands your full attention – it could be taxing like a maths problem or something you'd love to think about, plan or make.

Your OCD will want you to dismiss these *thought displacements* quickly and get you back to your habitual obsessions and compulsions (just as when you fold your arms in an unhabitual way, part of you will want to get back to folding your arms the way you always have – back to your 'old habits'). At such moments, **never try to push the OCD away** (because that will only strengthen it – trying not to think of something doesn't work) instead **simply give your attention to these displacing thoughts** – *the holiday, the Christmas gifts, maths problem, the paradox, the musical calculation, or the newly written joke, the mood-board, or contemplating the next five years* - that you have chosen to focus on.

While you are focussing on these 'displacers,' make sure that you remove yourself from the place where the OCD usually persists. You might not like it at first – it will feel like folding your arms the wrong way - but it will get easier. Here are a few things to look out for which will help you:

- Notice in which moments specifically you feel compelled towards a set of OCD rituals. What situations act as triggers for you? Where are you when you usually give in to your compulsions?

- *At the very moment you feel compelled*, remember to remove yourself physically from the situation. Force yourself to walk away. If you cannot physically remove yourself (e.g. you have to stay at your work desk) then remove yourself mentally and emotionally. Think different thoughts and feel different feelings.

- At this point, OCD is likely to nag you – *if you let it* – **but with thought displacers, you can deal with it.**

The biggest gains are in the mind, attitudes and practices of the sufferer.

> Do the thing you fear and the death of fear is certain.
>
> Ralph Waldo Emerson

Knowing the technique of **thought displacement** could be the key to your progress, but **thought displacement** is useless, *unless you put it into practice every time.*

Objections to Thought Displacers

By their very nature, **Thought Displacers** will not, at first, feel comfortable. But **Thought Displacement** represents a change which has the power to evict the Unwanted Guest (eventually) – and naturally the Guest (OCD) *would much rather things stayed the same.*

If you choose to remain obsessed and focussed on your usual habits then you will feel compelled to satisfy (give in to) these obsessions and this will simply make things worse. You don't get rid of a hungry monster by feeding it.

> Compulsions are a lousy solution to the problem of having obsessions.
>
> Fred Penzel

Some sufferers might think my advice obvious, but it is only as obvious as showing a desert traveller where they can find water. If the water is *there*, why would anyone send them elsewhere?

It is only when you practice **Thought Displacement**, when you make it a habit (*at the very moment when you would usually feel obliged to follow your compulsions*) that you will feel the benefit. If you use it *every time*, then it will serve you well. Slowly, you will start to defeat the tired routine. It is not easy (especially at first) but it becomes easier with practise.

I developed the ***Thought Displacement Technique*** to help clients suffering from OCD to get relief from the circular obsessive thought patterns which become maddening and distressing. This technique alone has given many sufferers back their freedom (the eviction of the unwanted guest). Despite its efficacy, *it will often be resisted by OCD sufferers.*

There is a useful story concerning the importance of placing our efforts where we will get the most leverage:

An old man was walking home late one night down a darkened street. The street lamps were quite far apart. As the man walked he stopped, sneezed and pulled a handkerchief from his trouser pocket. As he did so he inadvertently spilled lots of coins which fell clanking to the ground. Then he did something strange. He walked a few yards back to a lamp post and started scrutinizing the pavement. He was furtively looking all around the base of the lamp post but finding nothing.

Now it happened that a passer-by on the other side of the road had witnessed the event, and she was puzzled when she saw him looking in the wrong place for his coins. She crossed the road to help him.

"Excuse me sir," she said. "I think you dropped your money over there." She pointed to the spot where the man had sneezed. The man's answer surprised her-

"Oh, I know that," the man said. "But the light is much better here."

It is easier to just give in to old habits, but you will not find any answers there. It *is* easier to see under the clear light of a street lamp, *but that is not where your coins are.* It is easier to follow your OCD - you already know the script - *but there are no answers there*.

There is tremendous leverage in the **Thought Displacement Technique** – huge gains are to be found in its practice – even if the light seems better by just giving in to your OCD.

The Critical Moment

If you are an OCD sufferer you have to understand that no one else can fix this for you. You have to do it yourself. That may sound frightening, but I would prefer you to see it as empowering because you really can fix it. This book will give you a greater understanding and lots of guidance and tips, but in the end it will be what you DO that makes the difference – or even what you DON'T DO. Your commitment to positive change is vital.

The good news is that there are specific times throughout the day when your efforts will make a huge difference to your progress. These Critical Moments relate to the concept of leverage - which is about our effort having a maximum effect. So where are these critical moments where a little effort makes a big difference? They are precisely at the instant when we want to move from healthy behaviour to OCD behaviour. For example, we wash our hands *(which is healthy)* and then we feel that we want to wash them again immediately *(which is unhealthy)*. <u>At that precise moment</u>, we need to walk away. This is the moment when our efforts will be most rewarded, this is where we will start to regain our lives, this is the moment where we will defeat OCD. If you like, this is OCD's most vulnerable spot. You need to exploit it to regain your identity, your free-will and your life.

> The longer we dwell on our misfortunes, the greater is their power to harm us.
>
> Voltaire

Once we entertain the possibility of remaining at the sink (for example) and washing our hands again, we are flirting dangerously with the idea of handing over our lives to OCD. This is not about washing our hands a second time, this is about handing over control of our lives to something *which prefers you to be a robot and not a human* – namely OCD.

When we looked earlier at the difference between *not doing, doing and over-doing*, I was really drawing attention to the fact that when we move from *doing* to *over-doing* – that's precisely the moment when we are feeding (and growing) our OCD – that is the *critical moment*. If we become aware of it, and we consciously notice the threshold between healthy and unhealthy behaviour, then we have a choice as to what we want to do.

OCD would have us believe that we *have to* entertain it, to do as it commands, follow it, etc. But we can, if we are mindful of what is happening, choose to walk away having already done what we needed to do. We can move away from an unhealthy choice to a healthy choice.

It is at these moments that you will defeat your OCD. These critical moments are where the leverage is.

> If you don't get uncomfortable leaving your comfort zone, then you haven't really left it.
>
> Tim Brownson

As with any new habit, you may not feel comfortable at first, but if you use the thought displacers, then you will be focussing on a different direction, absorbed by new thoughts. In that moment, you will be freed from the tyranny of your obsessions.

OCD and Paranoia

OCD is a liar. It tells you that if you don't follow a set of mindless rituals, then disaster will strike. However, it has no real evidence that this is so. Consequently it has to ascribe catastrophic meanings to innocent things: a slight bump in the road when you are driving to work means that you definitely ran over a pedestrian; a plug switched off at the wall, without the plug being removed from the socket becomes the source of an imagined fire which rages out of control and kills hundreds of people.

Because there isn't enough evidence out there of real dangers, that you are actually neglecting, OCD has to misinterpret and catastrophize. Without these gross misperceptions, OCD would never be convincing. In this way, ordinary, safe occurrences are invested with dark significances. The sufferer has learned to terrorise themselves. They have been taken in by the unfounded hysterics of a liar; they have become the slaves of OCD.

> A black cat crossing your path signifies that the animal is going somewhere.
>
> Groucho Marx

As a teenager I got a job in the local co-op supermarket stacking shelves and delivering groceries. At the end of each Saturday some produce would be thrown away because the sell-by dates were too short. I asked if I could take them instead. There were a few tinned goods, some bread and a few other items. I put them in a small box and on my way home went to the house of an elderly lady who lived alone nearby. When she opened the door I was still wearing my Co-op jacket. When I told her about the goods and their short sell-by dates she asked *who sent me.* I explained that no-one sent me and that I just thought she might like some free groceries. She then asked me *what was in them.* Then she got very angry and insisted that I was just like the rest of them. She slammed the door in my face and saddened by her response, I took the groceries home for my own family. What I didn't realize was that the woman was schizophrenic.

Schizophrenia is not the same as OCD, but the paranoid misinterpretation of ordinary situations is very similar. So too is the ability to see dangers where there are none. Malevolent meanings are ascribed to innocent events. In the case of OCD, it is all in service to the narrative that something disastrous has happened or will happen. This, of course, is a lie.

> I have not ceased being fearful, but I have ceased to let fear control me. I have accepted fear as part of life, specifically fear of change and fear of the unknown;
> and I have gone ahead despite the pounding in the heart that says, turn back, turn back, you'll die if you venture too far.
>
> Erica Jong

OCD invokes Fight-or-Flight

Our *useful* fight-or-flight response
If we were walking through the jungle and we saw a tiger stalking us, we would naturally be afraid. Our bodies would produce the following symptoms:

- Increase in heart rate
- Increase sweat
- Jaw may lock
- Adrenaline and cortisol dumped in the bloodstream
- Blood goes to arms and legs (away from major organs)
- Trembling / shaking

This is our fight-or-flight response. We feel very anxious and we are being prepared for battle or running away.

In the case of meeting a tiger face-to-face, this is a useful response – it helps us in an emergency.

Our *useless* fight-or-flight response
If we are sitting at home relaxing or out at the cinema and suddenly we start to worry about some imagined catastrophe, or we get anxious that we forgot to perform some simple task (in other words when we have OCD thoughts) our bodies will produce all of the fight-or-flight responses (the increased heart rate, the locked jaw, etc.). This is not only unhelpful, it's useless. There is NO tiger. So what *feels* like a life or death situation is only *us frightening ourselves.* It is like being

afraid of the fear (which makes us more afraid). It becomes a vicious circle, feeding on itself. We feel anxious – it makes us frightened – then we get more anxious.

Whenever I allow OCD to *scare me*, whenever I *resist it*, whenever I *try to get control* – I WILL ACTUALLY BE INCREASING THE FIGHT-OR-FLIGHT RESPONSE

What to do instead when you feel the onset of OCD
Say to yourself:

- I'm having OCD thoughts right now, but that's okay, I accept it
- I'm not going to add to my fear
- It will pass
- I will not resist it
- My mind and body believe there is some big danger, but there isn't so I'm not going to react
- I may feel bad for a moment, but it will pass
- It will be silly if I get anxious about feeling anxious
- There are no tigers here

If you do this, you will experience success and soon you will reprogram your mind. In time you will feel at ease; you will realize and know *'I've been here before and it went great.'*

OCD will begin to stop when you can tell yourself that something is no longer a danger and that in fact, you have imagined a danger out of all proportion.

OCD – The Mind-Parasite

> Pain of mind is worse than pain of body.
>
> Publius Syrus

OCD is not a parasite in the biological sense of the term, but it may help to think of it as a parasite (in the psychological and emotional sense). Indeed, such a metaphor may give us a better sense of perspective when it comes to understanding our co-habitation with this *Unwanted Guest.*

When birds peck at fish from the water surface, the fish have an instinctive reflex to dive down to the depths. However there are certain parasites in sticklebacks *(Schistocephalus solidus)* which cause them to remain near the surface even when birds peck at them. The parasites within the fish have altered their hosts' survival instincts. The parasites need to be eaten by birds as part of their life cycle. All parasites alter the behaviour of their hosts to suit their own needs. How they do it is not yet understood.

There is another parasite, a fungus called *cordyceps,** which sometimes uses ants as its host. Any ant infected will be taken over by the parasite, causing the ant to climb to the highest part of a plant and bite down on a branch or stem. Here it will die and a fungal tendril will emerge from its body (usually its head) whereupon it releases more cordyceps spores that will be carried on the wind to infect further ants.

OCD is like a parasite – *a mind-parasite* – and like all parasites it alters its host's behaviour to suit its own ends. OCD reduces the person to something like an automaton, a robot, a mindless set of routines and procedures.

Life becomes a tramline of predictability and *meaning* is lost. The person finds comfort in the routine. They become convinced that they are *preventing danger* and that if they don't attend to their routines that disaster will strike. Anticipated dangers are exaggerated out of all proportion by OCD and the anxiety of the threat provides the engine for mindless reiterating procedures. A life subjugated, if we let it, a life lost.

If OCD were a *physical* parasite (like a hookworm, a threadworm, tapeworm or liver fluke) it would be possible to do a parasite cleanse using Wormwood, Black Walnut and Cloves.

But how do we rid ourselves of a *mind* parasite? Is it possible to do a mind-parasite cleanse?

Yes it is, and the way it is done is surprisingly playful.

---

* There are many varieties of *cordyceps* and they affect a whole host of insects including caterpillars.

Surreal Thoughts

Tremendous gains often come from doing the opposite of what OCD wants us to do. Parasite-infected sticklebacks would benefit enormously - *they would live* - if they could oppose their newfound compulsion to remain near the water surface.

However, when you oppose your OCD it doesn't need to be direct or painful. Indeed I am not fond of the *no pain, no gain* maxim, I think it makes life a discipline when it could be a dance. So how do we do this *mind-parasite* cleanse?

It works like this. OCD wants you to become a robot, it wants you to subjugate all possibilities to pre-set procedures; to narrow down your options to well-worn routines, to dull your life into a monochrome of predictability.

As with the stickleback example, it is worth thinking about what the parasite *does and doesn't want* you to do.

OCD wants you to:

- Be anxious about life
- Be predictable and endlessly risk-assessing
- Only use creativity for imagining disasters
- Stick to your routines and never deviate
- Narrow down your emotions to just two – fear and anxiety

At this point it would be worth checking if this mind-parasite has got you doing what it wants? Has it turned you into a comfortable host? You might be alarmed if you find that it has. So let's explore further ways you can rid yourself of this mind-parasite. Answers come if we examine what OCD doesn't want you to do.

OCD doesn't want you to:

- Be relaxed about life and living
- Be playful and enjoy possibilities
- Be imaginative (except when imagining danger and catastrophe)
- Change your routines
- Express a wide range of emotions (it mainly wants you to feel fearful and anxious)

If you were to develop these (in ways that were relaxed and playful) then you would be tackling OCD on a very deep level, by stealth as it were. You would begin to re-wire your brain and strengthen the likelihood of ridding yourself of OCD.

When we are children, our imaginations are amazing. We can play with a toy car around the leg of a table – and in that moment, the table leg is *a lamp post* or a *building*. We can drape a sheet over a few chairs and the enclosed space is now *a house*. Such powerful imaginations can be put to great use when we are older. We can see solutions which others are blind to. We can design new products, services and generate new ideas around any given subject. Sadly, most of us lose this ability as we develop into adulthood. The education system is a discouraging place for imaginative and creative children. Indeed each successive formal year of education reduces the scope of the enquiring imagination and the playful mind. Instead, most educational systems favour only high probability answers and conformist thinking. Yet imagination remains one of our highest faculties. Indeed, one of the greatest physicists who ever lived once said:

> Imagination is more important than knowledge.
>
> Albert Einstein

It was Einstein's imagination which gave us the *Special and General Theories of Relativity.* It began with what he called a 'thought-experiment' – a way of visualizing a situation. He imagined a car travelling at the speed of light, and then he wondered what would happen if the driver turned the headlights on. Would they shine? Would the speed of the car stop the light from ever being able to emerge from the headlights?

It is worth noting that people with OCD (without exception) *all have imaginative faculties* – after all they can picture so many dangers and visualize bad things happening. The difference is that they are not running their own imaginations. OCD is. It has taken charge.

The exercises which follow are ones which will help an OCD sufferer take back their own imaginative faculties - to reclaim that which is rightfully theirs. They will also encourage a more relaxed attitude toward life, a sense of playfulness and possibility, a change in routines and a wider range of emotions.

> IMPORTANT: **Do NOT do the following exercise if you suffer from psychotic episodes, schizophrenia or experience delusional hallucinations or similar, etc.**
> **See the disclaimer at the start of this book.**

The following exercises involve a daydream state wherein you can imagine surprising and enchanting things happening. *Do them at a slow, relaxed pace; pause in-between to absorb the changes you are witnessing.* Use your imaginative powers fully to visualize clearly and vividly, each new change. These exercises are designed to be playful and fun - similar to a childlike state. Keep them light and happy.

If it helps, you could have someone, whom you trust, guide you through this visualisation (i.e. they could read through it slowly whilst you close your eyes and visualize). Alternatively you could record yourself reading through it and play it back while you close your eyes and visualize. Be sure to do this exercise slowly. You need to fully *visualize* and *experience* the surreal changes as the exercise unfolds.

Exercise one:

First sit in a comfortable chair, or lie down. Take a deep breath and relax. Allow your eyes to feel heavy, and when you are ready, close them - as you settle deeply into a dreamy, pleasant state.

Picture your phone on a table.
Notice its colour, shape and size.
Now picture the phone slowly bending in half as if it were sitting up.
See the phone twisting as if to look around the room.
Now let the phone stand up.
Watch the phone float up and hover slowly six inches into the air.
See the space between the phone and the table.
Now have your phone slowly start to fly in circles around the room.
Now let it fly in a figure of eight.

Allow the phone to change colour to a completely different colour.
And then to another colour.
And now let it be multicoloured.
Notice the pattern the colours make.
Watch it 'land' somewhere on the ceiling.
Now watch it slowly inflate like a balloon until it is very round.
Now see this balloon-shaped phone slowly melt and drip onto the floor.
Eventually there is nothing left on the ceiling.
See the empty ceiling where the phone was.
Now see the drips on the floor come together.
Watch as the pieces slowly recreate your phone.
Now see your reconstituted phone 'stand up' and walk back towards the leg of the table it came from.
Allow the phone to slowly climb back up the table leg.
See your phone 'walk back' to the table top.
Watch it settle back to its exact starting position.
All is just as you first found it.

Take a deep breath and relax.
Slowly bring your attention back to this room.

Open your eyes and take a moment to reconnect with the external world.

I will offer a few more *Surreal Thoughts Exercises*, but it is not intended that you do them all at once; having said that, no harm will come from doing them that way. But, in the main, the exercises in this book work best when practised at regular intervals rather than all at once. One huge effort does not make a habit, only regular, consistent practice and repetition can do that. Slow and steady wins the race. In time it would be best if you could reclaim your own playful nature – and invent your own *Surreal Thought Exercises.* Here's another one:

Exercise two:

First sit in a comfortable chair, or lie down. Take a deep breath and relax. Allow your eyes to feel heavy, and when you are ready, close them - as you settle deeply into a dreamy, pleasant state.

Imagine your hand lying flat on a table.
Just resting.
Now watch as your little finger and the side of your hand pleasantly and slowly sinks into the table top.
You are safe and it is fun.
It feels comfortable and warm.
Gradually let the rest of your hand submerge.
Feel how pleasant it feels.
Now let your arm sink into the table.
The whole of one arm is now in the table.

Now let the rest of your body slowly and pleasantly sink into the table.

How interesting and funny it feels to *be* a table.

Now that you are in the table, look around and see what the table sees.

Allow your table to expand until it is as big as it can be in the room.

Now let your body seep out from underneath the table, and gently float to the floor.

Look up and see underneath the table.

This is a view you don't usually see.

Allow the table legs to become tree trunks.

Watch the branches grow.

You are safe. You are comfortable.

Let the table and the room become a vast forest.

You are perfectly safe.

Feel the beautiful quiet of the forest.

Enjoy the delightful stillness.

Now you can hear friendly birds singing.

You are pleasantly warm and happy.

Just allow those happy feelings to magnify and grow.

Allow some lovely sunlight to break through the forest.

Feel the warmth of the sun on your skin.

Allow the light to brighten.

In the bright light, the forest slowly disappears.
For a moment there is a pleasant nothingness.
Still with eyes closed, you see the room you were in slowly reappear around you.
You are happy.
Relax and breathe deeply.
There is nothing to do and nowhere to be.
Enjoy the relaxation.
Slowly bring your attention back to this room.
Open your eyes and take a moment to reconnect with the external world.

At this stage, you should simply be enjoying the playfulness of these guided visualizations. Give yourself to them. Be like a child again. It is good to allow yourself to think in ways which are counter to the usual OCD way.

Although these exercises might seem frivolous or even lightweight, I can assure you that they are indeed *a very useful part* of your road to freedom. In the next chapter I shall explain why these exercises are so important to OCD sufferers.

But for now, here's another one:

Exercise three:

First sit in a comfortable chair, or lie down. Take a deep breath and relax. Allow your eyes to feel heavy, and when you are ready, close them - as you settle deeply into a dreamy, pleasant state

In your mind see a shoal of friendly fishes swim into the air in the room.
Watch as they swim around.
They are beautiful.
Notice how their colours catch the light as they change direction.
Allow them to swim around for a while.
While the fish are swimming, notice a cup rising and floating up to join them.
All swimming together playfully - happy.
The cup swims inbetween the fish.
Your shoes become brightly coloured.
They develop long, pretty fins.
You see yourself float up, and swim with them.
Feel yourself glide through the water.
You breathe easily.
Safe and happy.
You and the shoal of fish swim close together.
Now slowly you turn into a beautiful fluffy white cloud.
The fishes gently fade.
You see a clear blue sky.
Enjoy drifting.
You drift over a beautiful lake.
Then you become rain falling.
See yourself dripping.
Carried on the wind.

Dripping down into the lake.
You become one with the lake.
You are connected to the whole of nature.
You support the fishes, the birds and the whole eco-system.
The whole of nature is within you.
Rest a while.
Now allow yourself to be back where you always were.
Back in your body.
Back here.
In the Now.
All is well.
Slowly, in a moment, open your eyes.
Open your eyes.
Take a deep breath and relax.
Slowly bring your attention back to this room.
Take a moment to reconnect with the external world.

Notice how these exercises felt. It is the *experience* of them which is important.

In a world dominated by adult logic and sensibility, it is very valuable to have moments where we can experience play and playfulness. Some adults might even be so far from this important experience that they shun the very idea or experience discomfort when trying the previous exercises. It might well be the case that the more you dislike them, the more you need them.

Here's some useful advice from the White Queen in *Alice Through the Looking Glass*:

"I'm just one hundred and one, five months and a day."
"I can't believe that!" said Alice.
"Can't you?" the Queen said in a pitying tone. "Try again: draw a long breath, and shut your eyes."
Alice laughed. "There's no use trying," she said: "one *can't* believe impossible things."
"I daresay you haven't had much practice," said the Queen.
"When I was your age, I always did it for half-an-hour a day. **Why, sometimes I've believed as many as six impossible things before breakfast.**"

Alice through the Looking Glass (Chapter 5)
by Lewis Carroll
(Illustration by Sir John Tenniel)

What's so good about surrealism?

These *Surreal Thoughts Exercises* are designed to help OCD sufferers to experience the difference between *reality* and *fantasy*. They are so fanciful and imaginative that it should be easy to distinguish them as fantasy (and not reality).

They remind the OCD sufferer that just because we vividly imagine something, it doesn't make it true. They also encourage a person to take charge of their imagination – each line of each exercise guides the person to visualize fanciful transformations one increment at a time.

> It could be argued that OCD is nothing more than an out of control imagination which serves up one imagined catastrophe after another; a runaway dark-fantasy which is in a constant state of hysteria – and which elicits a fight-or-flight response for *every **imagined*** problem.

Taking charge of that imagination is a decision that you can make. The *Surreal Thoughts Exercises* give you a framework by which it can be done.

One of the major issues for someone with OCD is that they tend to connect thoughts *(the imagined world)* very tightly with actions *(the real world)*. They do this in at least three ways:

1. If they think of (imagine) something which could go wrong, they immediately feel that they *alone* are responsible for preventing this catastrophe.

2. They think that they are responsible for any negative thought (any imagined trauma) which enters their mind. But as we have seen, we are not responsible for the thoughts which enter our heads. What we are responsible for is those thoughts we hang on to, those we stay stuck on, those we choose to replay over and over.

3. They give a thought (something they imagine) precisely the same weight as an action. For example... *'I hope I didn't run over any cyclists as I drove to work'* becomes *'I must check the car for damage to see if I killed anyone this morning without realising.'* For some, it has even led to them surrendering themselves to the police because they have convinced themselves that they must have injured or killed someone.

These examples all illustrate that thinking is being treated *as if every thought were a manifestation*, as if every thought must be acted upon instead of simply remaining as just a thought. The *Surreal Thoughts Exercise* helps break the link between thought and actions. It demonstrates to the thinker that thoughts alone are safe; that we can have thoughts which lead to no actions whatsoever. In fact, we can have thoughts which will never lead to anything except a happy, childlike playfulness and a great sense of freedom.

It is also common for people suffering from OCD to assume that others can read their thoughts. This too is a symptom of their belief that thoughts are things - that thoughts are out there - and not just inside their own heads.

When we learn a new thing or do things differently, we form new neural pathways. These become strengthened with use. I am not just speaking metaphorically; I am talking about actual physical changes in the brain. It is said that 'Neurons which fire together will wire together.' The stronger pathways then become the default. The saying 'you can't teach an old dog new tricks' is just another way of saying that the default pathway becomes the established norm.

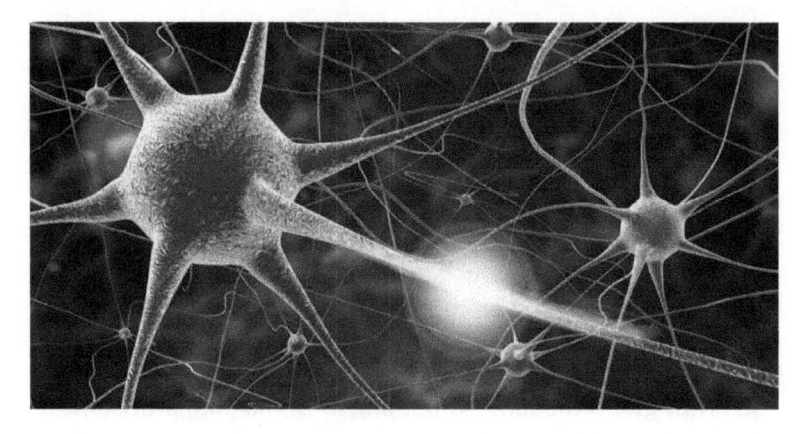

In time, the obsessive thoughts and compulsive behaviours of OCD will cause changes in the brain, creating super-highways for bad habits. The 'roads' for free will, imagination, creativity and playfulness will fall into disrepair and become 'unadopted.' We could look at it this way:

The Neurons that we habitually fired
Have become our choices - *hard-wired.*

The remedy? *Surreal Thoughts Exercises* and *Thought Displacers!* The repetition of good habits will strengthen *those* neural pathways, eventually making *them* the super-highways. In this way, a new default neural pathway will have been established. Remember that *habit is overcome by habit.*

With the *Surreal Thoughts Exercises* you are teaching your brain to make connections *counter to those OCD wants to make.* Imagine being automatically creative and imaginative, instead of automatically compelled to follow the dull and boring thoughts of OCD. These exercises, together with other ideas and training in this book, are designed to restore that which has been buried by OCD – namely the fully human being or the sovereign you. The aim is to rediscover the happy adventure of living.

Let's explore the biological efficacy of the claims I am making. As with most of the body, cells die in the brain and new ones are formed. But in the brain, the priority is according to use. In this way, our thoughts and feelings affect the physical structure of the brain. This is known as *neuro-plasticity.*

Our brains use chemicals called neurotrophins which help to make healthy connections in nerve cells. Neurotrophins (like BDNF: Brain Derived Neurotrophin Factor) can actually grow new neural pathways for us, and amazingly, *these are formed according to what thoughts and feelings we choose.* In this sense, mind really does affect matter.

Another vital and similar chemical, called Pro-BDNF, kills brain cells and breaks down unwanted connections. In this sense, another old saying is true *'If you don't use it, you lose it'* and this is as true of OCD as it is of neural pathways. If you feed OCD every day, you will simply get more OCD and it will become the norm, hard-wired into your way of thinking. But the good news is that, with *neuro-plasticity*, you can create new pathways (with new thinking) and remove old, unwanted pathways (simply by deliberate neglect).

It doesn't matter how long you have had OCD or how old you are, the brain by its very nature is neuro-plastic and eminently changeable. If you stop thinking OCD thoughts then *Pro-BDNF* will slowly kill off those pathways. If you habitually think different thoughts, then *BDNF* will work to strengthen those new pathways. You won't lose your general sense of safety, but you will lose your obsessions and compulsions. You won't be a slave anymore.

These new neuro pathways, which can be established by the *Thought Displacers* and *Surreal Thoughts* exercises, will make your brain a hostile environment for OCD. Healthier thinking will take its place with newly forged neuro pathways. *The unwanted guest* will have no choice but to leave. The conditions for the *mind-parasite* will have changed and it will not be able to stay.

Partners, Friends and Family

When you start to make changes for the better and manage to reduce or overcome your compulsive behaviour, you may find that some family members / partners remind you not to forget your rituals. Without meaning to, they might drive you back into your compulsive behaviours. It's not that they wish you any harm, but they may have got so used to making allowances for you, giving you more time, etc. that they find any change difficult.

If they resist you moving forwards without your OCD, then they might inadvertently pull you back into it. This phenomenon is more common than most people realise. Indeed, whenever we attempt to change, it is often the people closest to us who resist the change the most and hold us back. Sometimes they have got used to things being the way they are; sometimes they need to be the helper (co-dependency) and sometimes your change is viewed as a threat. If they are trapped in their own negative habits, then they might not want to see you making your positive strides towards a better life.

It is wise to let those closest to you know that you are moving away from your compulsions now and don't wish to be reminded of them. This only works in families who support one another.

It sometimes happens that those around you have begun to feel very secure and happy when they compare themselves with your OCD problems. In families, scape-goating is common and if you are the member defined as the 'one with a problem' then the others might wish it to stay that way. I mention this because I want you to be aware of potential pit-falls in your journey to being fully functioning and OCD free.

So if you have to just go it alone, then please do. Given the choice of continuing an unhealthy relationship or growing towards your best self, the latter should win every time. You have the right to move towards your goals – especially when they benefit not only you, but those around you too.

Bloom's Taxonomy

Some concepts from the field of Education can provide OCD sufferers with useful insights into the nature of their condition. In particular, there is a diagram which maps how we learn things which will give you strategies for dealing with your OCD. It can also provide insights on the reflexive nature of obsessive thoughts and the dehumanising quality of compulsive behaviours.

When teachers are training to be teachers they usually encounter something called *Bloom's Taxonomy* – a diagram depicting various predictable stages of cognitive development (see next page). In 1956, Benjamin Bloom, an educational psychologist, chaired a committee of educationalists who devised this table classifying the steps from low level (basic understanding) and high level (deeper understanding).

Bloom's Taxonomy (which is just a fancy word for *classifications*) is not about the cleverness, I.Q., or the functionality of any learner, but rather is a predictor of the way a person assembles their learning. Specifically it is about the way that we all begin (when we learn something new) with a shallow surface knowledge, before we progress towards a deeper understanding (which gives the whole subject more meaning). His model codifies the evolving nature of a learner's thinking skills as they develop in their understanding and progress in their awareness and abilities.

The full title of this table of classification is *Bloom's Taxonomy of the Cognitive Realm* (which is knowledge based). Bloom and his committee devised similar classifications for *the affective realm* (emotion based) and for *the psychomotor realm* (action based). However I shall simply refer to the taxonomy of the cognitive realm as 'Bloom's Taxonomy' for our purposes.

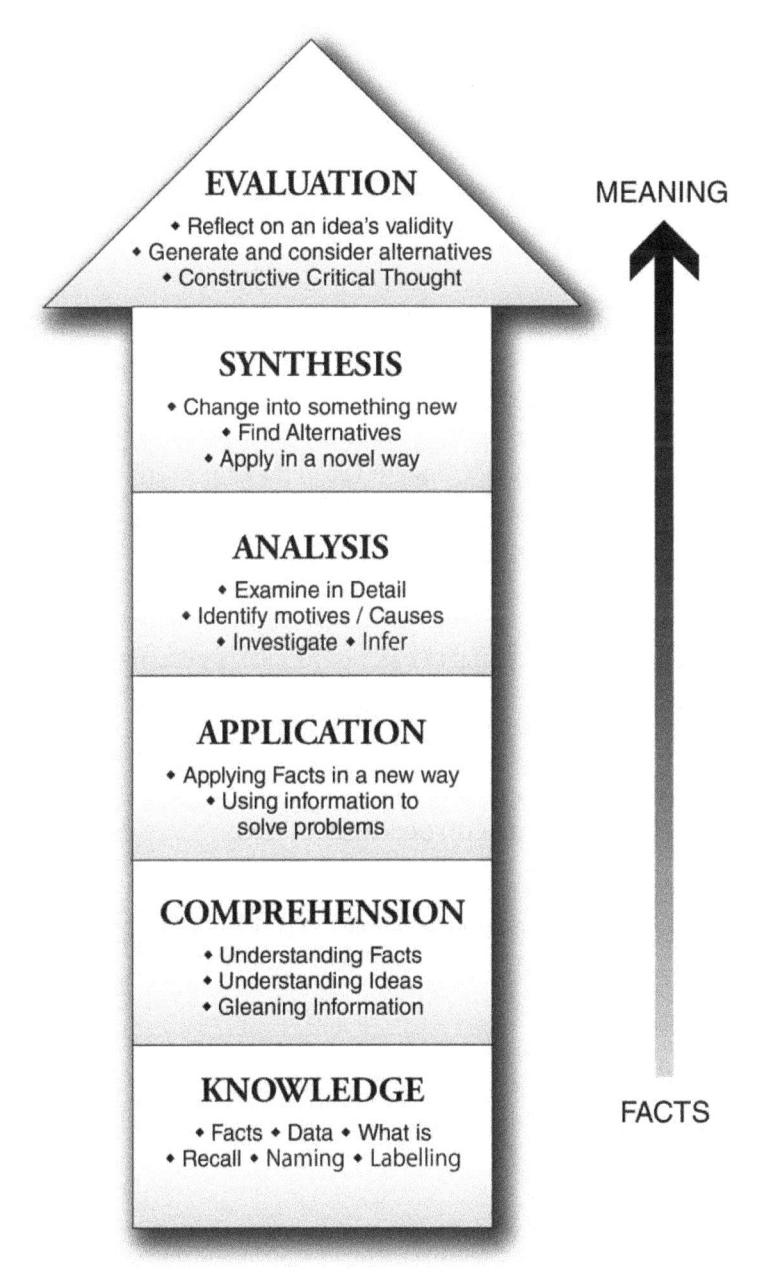

EVALUATION
- Reflect on an idea's validity
- Generate and consider alternatives
- Constructive Critical Thought

SYNTHESIS
- Change into something new
- Find Alternatives
- Apply in a novel way

ANALYSIS
- Examine in Detail
- Identify motives / Causes
- Investigate • Infer

APPLICATION
- Applying Facts in a new way
- Using information to solve problems

COMPREHENSION
- Understanding Facts
- Understanding Ideas
- Gleaning Information

KNOWLEDGE
- Facts • Data • What is
- Recall • Naming • Labelling

MEANING ↑ FACTS

So let's acquaint ourselves with this oddly named diagram. The diagram shows us that learning has a start point (Knowledge), but more importantly, *it has a direction.*

Knowledge

Let's take an example. Someone learning the guitar may learn that in standard tuning, the strings (from low to high) are tuned EADGBE. They might also start with naming the parts of a guitar: the frets, the neck, the headstock, the bridge, etc. We are on the level of *knowledge;* parts are being named and we become acquainted with 'what is.'

Similarly someone training to be a restaurant chef may first learn the different types of cutlery: a carving knife, a fish knife, a butter knife, a teaspoon, a tablespoon, a ladle, a long desert spoon, etc. At this level we are labelling things so that we might recall them at a later date. We are gathering data. At the *knowledge* level all we are doing is collecting data – we are not yet processing it (in the true sense) or applying it.

This level is a necessary stepping stone, but it quickly becomes very boring and tedious. Facts can be banal, and if we allow them to become devoid of meaning, they can be downright deceptive.

> There are three kinds of lies:
> lies, damned lies and statistics.
>
> Mark Twain's Own Autobiography:
> The Chapters from the North American Review

For example, Courts of Law the world over tend to operate from this low level (valuing *facts* over *meaning*). This is because Prosecutors and Defence teams are not interested in truth, their only priority is winning.

> **Prosecutor:** Did you or did you not leave the old lady in the burning house when you could have rescued her?

Defendant: Yes, I did but-
Prosecutor: *(interrupting)* –and is it true that she died in that house fire?
Defendant: Yes, but when-
Prosecutor: *(interrupting)* -and is it true that you chose not to rescue her?
Defendant: Yes, because-
Prosecutor: *(interrupting)* -and you admit that you *could* have rescued her?
Defendant: Yes, but there-
Prosecutor: *(interrupting)* -did she die as a result of your leaving her there to burn to death?
Defendant: Yes, but only bec-
Prosecutor: *(interrupting)* -So what you are saying is that you *knew* there was an old lady in the house, and that you *could* have rescued her *but you chose not to* – and because of your actions, she died.
Defendant: *(hesitating)*…Well, yes, but it was-
Prosecutor: *(interrupting)* Thank you. No further questions.

The Prosecutor, it seems, has got to the facts, and many would infer from the Defendant's unease that they are most likely to be guilty. After all, don't the guilty squirm and try to create excuses? Don't the guilty always dislike the *plain facts?*

In this particular case, it may surprise you to learn that what really happened was that the Defendant ran in to a burning house to rescue anyone inside. He knew an old lady lived there. That evening she was babysitting two toddler twins. Hearing their cries, he found them first in a smoke filled room, scooped them up and immediately carried them out to safety (leaving them in the arms of two neighbours). Then the Defendant ran back into the house to rescue the old lady, but was beaten back by the flames and the smoke.

Only now does the account have *meaning*. Now you can see how over-rated 'facts' can be. After all, the fact is that *the defendant did leave an old lady to die in a burning house when he could have rescued her.* This *is* true. It *is* an undeniable fact. Of course, the Defendant could have entered the burning house and ignored the toddlers completely (leaving them to die) and just saved the old lady instead. It was an impossible choice, and it might just be that on the level of *knowledge*, this person could be prosecuted for whoever they couldn't save. This is the blinkered view given to us if we remain at this banal level – innocent, brave people are deemed to be guilty cowards deserving incarceration. Facts can be partial, lacking context, devoid of true meaning. In this way they can be very dangerous, condemning us to an unreal world of banality.

And of course this level, the *knowledge* level, is the place where OCD resides. It is about facts which no longer have meaning, facts out of context, mindless procedures which no longer serve any meaningful purpose.

Knowledge is the level of the robot-mind; the collector, the hoarder. If we stay at the level of *knowledge*, we may even deceive ourselves into thinking that we are in a good place. But *knowledge* is like a bus stop, it is a great place to start, but a poor place to stay. Just as locking your car is a good thing to do, but not if you have to stay there checking you locked it again and again and again. Of course, an OCD sufferer would argue that it is a *fact* that it is good to check your car is locked – and like the prosecutor in the previous example, they can be right, but only partially. Their 'rightness' may be concealing deceptive or toxic behaviour.

To be right only in a very narrow way - and not to take in all the evidence is another kind of foolishness.

> I am but mad north-north-west
>
> Shakespeare (Hamlet Act 2, Scene 2)

The *knowledge* level is a barren waste if we don't move to higher levels. It is worthless compared to the higher levels. It may be a great place to start, but it is a very poor place to end.

Comprehension

When we move to the level of *comprehension* we are able to understand the differences we have learned. We can summarise what we know. We have a basic understanding of the facts and ideas we have been exposed to. We can explain what we know to someone else. On a basic level, we understand what the facts mean.

Application

The level of *application* it is like a quantum leap as we move toward higher level thinking. We can now start to use our knowledge and understanding. We *apply* what we have learned to answer new questions, to deal with a wide variety of situations. At this level we begin to solve problems. We generalise from what we know and comprehend. At this level our map of know-how broadens and we become more resourceful. We have learned to apply facts, rules and ideas.

Analysis

At the level of *analysis* we tend to examine things in greater detail. We may ask 'What are the parts of this?' We may also ask 'What is this a part of?' We are looking at relationships as well as things. We begin to infer conclusions from our analysis. We may look at causes, motives, or evidence to support or refute previous generalisations. We might compare things in a new way; we might reorganise our ideas. Components are given greater scrutiny whether they are facts, rules or ideas.

Synthesis

At the level of *synthesis* we are using very high level thinking skills. We are now able to use learning from one frame of reference and use it in a new way to solve a completely different problem. We may combine elements in completely new ways; we might perceive a brand new use for something. When mathematicians read a prose problem and see that it requires simultaneous equations to solve the problem, then they are using synthesis. A narrative has been *synthesised* into algebra.

At *synthesis* we combine elements in new ways, we find new patterns and we transfer our skills into new areas. We adapt, shape and modify rules and concepts to originate new things, ideas and perceptions. This is the level of invention, design and creativity. At this level we play, experiment, challenge the norm, and we oppose the cliché and forge something original and new.

This level is generative and divergent, as opposed to the level of *knowledge* which was merely sterile and convergent.

I witnessed a great example of *synthesis* when a fashion designer who was also a great tailor gave a talk to some Art and Design students I was teaching. During Q and A at the end of his presentation a student asked him a question. The exchange went something like this:

> **Student:** I love your work and you seem to be able to almost think in 3D; it's as if you can look at a flat ream of cloth and see how it would work in the round on a model. Where did you learn that?
>
> **Fashion Designer:** Actually, my answer for that may strike you as unusual, but it's the truth... I live near the Peak District and used to work every summer building and mending dry-stone walls, and I don't know if you know this but when you build a dry-stone wall you pick up a rock from your pile and you find a place where it will fit. You NEVER put it down if it doesn't seem to fit anywhere, you rotate it and turn it *until* you find a fit. Otherwise you'd be handling lots of rocks twice and making a second a pile of rocks (of rocks-that-don't-fit-walls). And in some way, a way that I can't fully explain, this dry-stone walling gave me a sense of three dimensions. Somehow this business of thinking in three dimensions and rotating these rocks until I could *see* a fit gave me what I needed for relating flat drapery to 3D figures.

This is the essence of *Synthesis*; applying learning from one frame of reference to a completely different area and in a novel way. It is also about having the inner resources and flexibility of thinking to perceive and make such connections.

Evaluation

The level of *evaluation* is the highest level in *Bloom's Taxonomy*. It is the level at which we step back and reflect on our opinions, ideas, judgements and consider their validity and quality. We are evolved enough to be self-critical (in a constructive way) to weigh what we have and consider the possibility of error, or the invalidity of our position. Even when our position is robust, we might still consider improvement and contemplate alternatives.

At the level of evaluation we are able to step back and look at where we are, what we have made, what we are doing, etc. And question its efficacy, validity and value. We are looking for improvements rather than merely trying to find faults.

Let's take a useful metaphor:

> A man with an axe was chopping wood by a country road-side. It was a hot day, the sun was high and he had sweat stains on his shirt. The axe was rusty and blunt. A woman in a pick-up truck pulled over nearby.
> "Hey, I saw you struggling with that axe and I thought I'd stop because I have an axe sharpener on the back of my truck. If you run that rusty ol' blade through it a few times, you'll get through that woodpile like it was butter. No charge." She smiled and squinted into the sun.
> The man looked at her like a parent with an exasperating child:
> "Do you think I've got time to stop and talk to you? Can't you see all this wood I've got to chop?"
> "Yes. But if you stop for just a moment, you'll have a sharper axe and you'll get through all that wood in no time."

"Look, I've got work to do. If you don't mind, I'd be grateful if you'd just leave me to it."

The woman shook her head in disbelief, walked back to her truck and opened the hot metal door, climbed in and drove off. In a few moments she was just a dot in the heat-haze at the end of a long dust trail. The man lined up the next block of wood and swung his axe heavily. With each swing he hardly made any impression. It was going to be a long afternoon. There was no doubt about it, he was working very hard.

Sharpening the axe would be working *smart* instead of *hard*.

People who don't reach the level of *evaluation* are condemned to work *in the business* without ever working *on the business*. They cannot innovate or reflect.

That is also the plight of the OCD sufferer, they cannot reflect on what they are doing – and the thought of contemplating doing something different is usually frightening.

But if we are ever to grow, then we all must contemplate other ways of approaching things:

> None may arrive at the Truth unless they are able to think that the path itself may be wrong.
>
> Ali, Son of the Father of the Seeker
> (Sufi Mystic writings Edited by Idries Shah)

In the next chapter we will consider how all this applies to OCD specifically.

Bloom's Taxonomy and OCD

Now that we have a good overview of *Bloom's Taxonomy,* we can see at a glance (see diagram on next page) that as we move up the levels we move from *What* to *How* to *Why*. As we advance, our learning becomes more enriched and more valuable. The direction of our learning has taken us from *facts* to *meaning*.

At the level of *knowledge*, someone could rightly assert that a book of Shakespeare's Hamlet was merely *black marks on white paper* - and in their own terms, they would be right. It *is* first and foremost black marks on white paper. As we move up the continuum of Bloom's Taxonomy we will discover higher and richer descriptions. As we move from *knowledge* to *evaluation* our understanding of what it is we are investigating becomes more real, more meaningful. From basic to sophisticated, we may discover (in sequence):

- The black marks are not random. It is *some kind of a code or language.*
- It is *something written in the English Language.*
- It is *a story* written in the English Language.
- It is a story written in *the form of a theatrical play* to be performed with actors as well as read.
- It is a *story set in Denmark in the form of a theatrical play* to be performed with actors as well as read.

And we could go on by increments until we arrive at much higher descriptions:

- It is the story or a university student, Hamlet, whose father has died suspiciously while he was away and whose mother married his uncle very hastily. A ghost appeared to him claiming to be his dead father. He told Hamlet that he was murdered and insists that Hamlet avenge his murder by killing his uncle. Hamlet is in a quandary. Can he believe the word of a ghost? Was his father really murdered? Did his mother conspire? The play charts his inability to act and his overactive mind as he weighs up his options, etc.

You will notice that we are now a very long way away from just *black marks on white paper.* However we must remember that *all of these statements are true*, it's just that the higher ones are always *richer and more meaningful.* Some might even say that at the higher levels, our perceptions, inquiry and conclusions are more *human.* They are not only more *true*, they are more *real*.

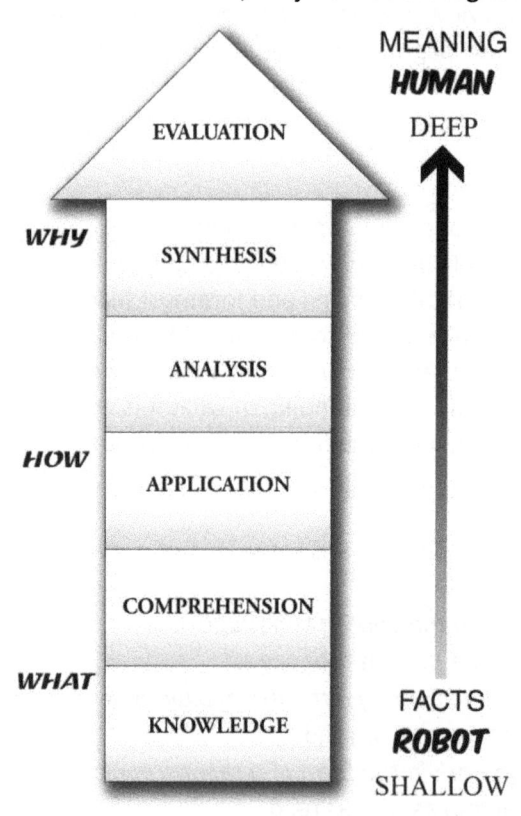

At the lower levels our scope is limited and we concern ourselves with shallow labels, procedures and routines. OCD favours the robot-mind. The question is: would you want to stay at the level of *Knowledge*, knowing as you do now that there is so much more?

Pyramid diagram with levels from bottom to top: KNOWLEDGE, COMPREHENSION, APPLICATION, ANALYSIS, SYNTHESIS, EVALUATION. Left side labels: WHAT, HOW, WHY. Center arrow pointing up with labels: SHALLOW / ROBOT / FACTS at bottom, DEEP / HUMAN / MEANING at top.

At this point you may have noticed that the *surreal thoughts* exercises are at the *synthesis* level. They take existing knowledge of things (fish, phones, etc.) and apply it in new ways (e.g. a cup can swim, a balloon can melt and drip).

When we move up Bloom's taxonomy, we are encouraging more neural connections. OCD prefers you to use fewer. It wants you to strengthen the few, rather than include the many. OCD keeps the sufferer on the level of *knowledge* – a robot insisting that this banal level makes sense.

When you move upwards beyond the level of *knowledge*, then you are growing in the direction of a more human life, a more meaningful existence – away from the shallow robot-mind of OCD.

OCD and Responsibility

Playfulness is the enemy of OCD. OCD is a Health and Safety officer on super steroids who believes that every playground should be closed, every sport should be banned, and no child should ever play out - after all, think of the risks! OCD only sees dangers, risks and problems. The world of benefits, fun, utility and laughter are unavailable to OCD.

Find activities you can do just for fun, and do them without turning them into compulsions or 'have-to's.' Build your playfulness. This involves being child-like again - after all, the creative adult is the one whose inner child survived. It is about re-connecting with your inner child. Each of the following exercises will help you to create new neural pathways which are vital if you are to reclaim that which has been lost to OCD. See how many you can do:

> *Exercise 1:* Play keepy-up with a balloon in your living room.
>
> *Exercise 2:* Fill saucepans with different levels of water and try to play a tune by tapping each one with a spoon (add/remove water to achieve the required notes).
>
> *Exercise 3:* Buy children's soap bubbles and sit in your back garden blowing them.
>
> *Exercise 4:* Pull faces in the mirror - try to express as many different emotions as you can.

Exercise 5: Go into every room of your house and take a moment to feel all of the different textures of things (the smoothness of furniture, the roughness of carpet-pile, the softness of a pillow).

Exercise 6: Pop some bubble-wrap. Sit down and really enjoy relaxing and popping.

Exercise 7: Using pen and paper, draw doodles and fill your sheet with images, symbols and patterns (they might be purely abstract or they might be representational in some way).

Exercise 8: Walk around the house like a chimpanzee. See if you can master that rolling gait and let your arms hang loose and low – how long can you do it for? How good is your impression?

Exercise 9: Re-read a story you loved as a child – if it was a picture book, really examine those pictures. Let yourself tumble into the story and immerse yourself with it as you once did.

Exercise 10: Put on some up-tempo music and dance around your room trying out many different dance styles. Imagine that you are proficient and crowds are applauding your moves. It might make you laugh.

The particular activities you choose here are not important. What is important is that you are *willing to do things that you thought you couldn't, shouldn't or mustn't.*

Where OCD is prohibitive, authoritative, and judgemental, your inner child is playful, free and joyful. OCD invents dangers which aren't there, whilst your inner child finds treasures which are.

One thing is certain, if you keep on doing what you've always done, you'll keep on getting what you've always got.

You have to do something different to get something different.

If you haven't noticed OCD's inner voice yet, listen for the one telling you:

> *"This is all very silly – I'd never do that!"*

It's that one.

Intensive Thinking

Earlier we looked at using new thoughts to replace unwanted (OCD) thoughts. If you recall, I suggested that it was futile to try to push away thoughts that you didn't want. That would only give them more energy and attention. As the saying goes, that which you resist will persist. Whatever you give your attention to will become more real. By far the best strategy is to take hold of thoughts you want and by giving them your full attention, unwanted thoughts (with practice) will evaporate.

The best thought displacers will absorb all of your attention, but they don't have to be complicated or mentally strenuous, just engaging and absorbing. In particular, it can be very effective to take an ordinary object and ponder it more thoroughly than ever before. I call this 'Intensive Thinking.'

Let's consider, for example:

A DECKCHAIR

- The fabric of a deckchair is usually striped. How wide are the stripes?
- How many stripes are there usually? Try to estimate.
- What shade of colours would these stripes be - bright poster colours? Muted earth colours? Faded pastel shades?
- If you zoomed in what would the texture of the fabric

- look like?
- What does the stitching pattern look like where the fabric wraps around the wooden frame?
- What shade is the wood?
- What type of wood do you think it is?
- How does the deckchair fold? Picture its geometry – which bit fits where?
- What pattern would it leave in the sand on a beach?
- What would lots of deckchairs on a beach look like from high up in the air? How different would they look when occupied compared to unoccupied?
- What would it be like to be a deckchair – what would you see when you were folded and stacked? Or when no one sat on you? Or when someone sat on you?

This type of *intensive thinking* is alien to most people. Indeed most people are poor *thinkers*. Western education systems reward speed rather than scope. They have made a nation full of fast drivers who are not very good at steering. A mind is too powerful an organ to never learn how to 'steer' it.

When an OCD thought intrudes, it usually wants you to act upon it. If you dwell on it (if you spend time with it) you will lose. When you give in to it, it will want more. If you entertain it, it will take over. If you try to push it away, you will connect with it even stronger. If you resist, it will persist. If you give it attention, it will grow. When such thoughts fly into our heads, that's the precise moment to indulge in some *intensive thinking* – **about something totally unconnected!**

In the above example we *thought intensely* about a deckchair, but you could give your attention to almost anything. Here's a brief list of possible subjects:

- A flag
- A sandwich
- A shoe
- A tin of paint
- A book
- A pen

- ❖ A beach ball
- ❖ A fishing rod
- ❖ A tennis racquet
- ❖ A radiator
- ❖ A guitar
- ❖ A bird cage
- ❖ The wheel of a car
- ❖ A birthday cake
- ❖ Etc.

The subject itself doesn't matter, so feel free to invent your own; what does matter is your ability to ponder that subject from many different angles, to develop a flexibility in thinking. This is useful not just to deal with unwanted thoughts, but also to exercise the mind – making it more perceptive and creative.

Once you have chosen a subject, here are a few prompts which might help you with your *intensive thinking:*

>Where does it come from?
>What is it made of?
>What are its colours?
>Are there any patterns?
>What is it like up close – zoomed in?
>Is it textured?
>What does it look like?
>What does it feel like?
>Is there a taste? Or a smell?
>What does it sound like?
>Does it have different parts? What is each like?
>How is it used? Is it part of a process?
>If I were the object, what would I see?

The deckchair example dealt with an examination of its intrinsic nature, with *what is,* but there is another form of *intensive thinking* which also works powerfully as a thought displacer. It occurs when we use our imaginations to challenge reality as we know it - when we ask *what if?*

To prove the point that intensive thinking does not have to be about something complex, let's choose a very humble subject as our starting point:

(thought bubble: A POTATO)

- What if potatoes didn't come from the ground – what if it rained potatoes?
- Perhaps we would run out and catch them?
- Would we need devices which looked like upturned umbrellas to catch them?
- Would rooftops and windows be made of stronger/different material?
- Would all windows have external shutters?
- Would rooftops be padded so you could sleep through a potato storm?
- What if potatoes had brightly coloured skins – red, yellow, green, blue, purple, etc?
- What if their skins were patterned with stripes or polka dots?
- What if they were different shapes – cubes, cones, cylinders, spheres, acorn shaped, etc?
- What if they bounced and you could play tennis with them?
- What if they could stretch like elastic?
- What if some were huge – a metre across?
- Etc.

Do you get the idea? Thinking in this playful way might seem very strange but there was a time when we all had the ability to think like this with ease – when we were children. Most people lose this facility as they mature, which is a shame because it is at the heart of all invention, innovation and ingenuity.

It is also how we all think each night when we surrender ourselves to sleep. In dreams, ordinary things are not subject to the usual laws of physics, and they don't need to behave according to type. While we sleep, potatoes might indeed display any of the properties we have imagined.

This *'what if'* type of *intensive thinking* is not only a lot of fun, but it is an incredibly powerful tool to use whenever you experience an unwanted OCD thought. It works best if you practice it.

Whether you consider *what is* or *what if*, you can use intensive thinking at the very moment OCD it at its most insistent. When OCD tries to control your thoughts, simply choose a possible subject from the previous list (i.e. a flag, a sandwich, a shoe, etc.) and think *intensely* about that instead.

It might not be easy at first, but it will become easier with practice. Remember – folding your arms the 'wrong way' is uncomfortable at first.

Habit can be used to overcome habit.

It's all about which wolf you choose to feed. The choice is yours.

Intensive thinking pulls you out of the rubble of the *knowledge* level of Bloom's taxonomy, helping you to be a creative human rather than a routine driven robot on auto-pilot.

You can't argue someone out of their OCD

With OCD, innocent phenomena become part of a conspiracy of evidences which prove that some catastrophe happened or is imminent. For example, a tiny surface scratch on a car door means that *I must have been in a terrible accident and not noticed*. In such cases, evidence to the contrary will not suffice. Indeed, it will only go to further the narrative that a catastrophe *has* occurred. OCD insists upon a worst case scenario. It takes all evidence and uses it against you.

A psychotherapist named Abraham Maslow (famous for formulating our *Hierarchy of Needs*) was once treating a client who believed he was a corpse. Maslow pointed out with good humour that not many corpses visit him but the man was undeterred.

"I know it sounds crazy but I am not speaking metaphorically. I am dead. I died a long time ago. I am here to see you, but I am in fact, a corpse."

Maslow had an idea:

"Do corpses bleed?"

"Of course they don't bleed. In corpses, the blood has congealed and the heart has stopped pumping – so no, corpses don't bleed."

Maslow took a small instrument – the sort used to check ketone levels for people with blood sugar problems. He asked the client if he would mind having the side of his finger pricked. The client said:

> "It doesn't matter to me one bit because I am a corpse – and anyway, corpses don't bleed."
> With that, Maslow pricked the side of the man's ring finger and a small drop of blood swelled and became a trickle. The man raised his hand to examine the burgundy blood as it slowly meandered down his finger and across his palm.
> "My god!" he said. "Corpses *do* bleed!"

Evidence to the contrary will never convince an OCD sufferer to abandon their compulsions because *OCD is not rational.* You can't argue the irrational back into 'normality' because it will use any evidence given to further its own case. Any new material will be used to further the sufferer's narrative.

> A patient once told a doctor that he had found a great way to keep mice from getting in his fridge:
> "I keep an old pair of shoes in there and it repels them."
> "But have you *ever* had mice in your fridge?" asked the doctor.
> "No, never. I told you it works! That's why I keep them there."

The Left and Right Brain

We are all born with a brain which has two distinct hemispheres. The left and right sides appear to have very different functions. We know this because:

1. People with head injuries on one side seem to suffer deficits which are very different to those of the other.

2. When the electrical activity of the brain is recorded during various tasks, different areas of the brain appear to be being used according to which task and function is being carried out. Electroencephalography (EEG) measures these voltage changes. Some tasks appear to utilize one hemisphere more than another and a pattern emerges.

3. People who suffer strokes have predictable deficits according to which side of the brain the blood blockage occurred.

4. People with brain diseases suffer problems relating to which hemisphere has been damaged the most.

Broadly speaking, each side of the brain is responsible for processing different types of information and dealing with different tasks.

On the following page is a diagram which broadly maps the characteristics of each hemisphere according to the tasks and processes it tends to handle most:

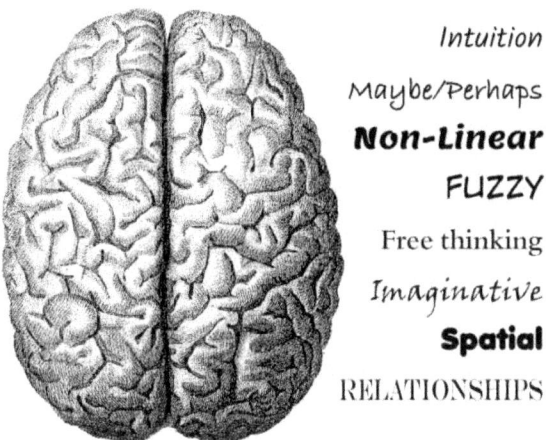

LEFT		RIGHT
Decisions		*Intuition*
Binary Yes/No		*Maybe/Perhaps*
Mathematical		**Non-Linear**
Logical		FUZZY
Reason		Free thinking
Language		*Imaginative*
Non Spatial		**Spatial**
Parts		RELATIONSHIPS

The above diagram is useful in general terms; however, we should be mindful that no one is fully 'right-brained' or 'left-brained.' For example, a gifted mathematician, would probably use creativity from the right hemisphere *as well as* logic and reason from the left. As we have seen, the brain shows tremendous plasticity and we always have choices. Nothing is fixed or determined.

In addition to this, we all have a fibrous tissue (the *corpus callosum*) which connects the two hemispheres and allows them to work together. This is sometimes referred to as the *'Rainbow bridge'* and it carries information across 250 million nerve fibres.

The brain is, of course, more mysterious than we can ever know, so I am not intending to over-simplify its function.[1] However the idea of different hemispheres having different, distinct functions has tremendous value - even if only as a metaphor – especially when it comes to OCD.

People often have a bias towards one side or the other – they spend more time living in one side of their brain. Some like to think of the left brain as being to do with the *Science and Linguistics* whilst the right could be said to do with the *Arts and Humanities*. Neither is better. There are advantages and disadvantages when either is dominant.

Let's consider *Left Hemisphere* dominance first:

Left Brain – Verbal and Sequential

Likely Advantages

- Would have good sequential memory
- Would be a good logical planner
- Would tend to have good reading and writing skills
- Will generally make steady and measurable progress
- Will experience that work delivers achievement
- Will have clear concept of boundaries
- Will be a logical thinker
- Prefers order and routine
- Often highly organised

Likely Disadvantages

- They tend to accept rather than work on difficulties
- They prefer to just repeat what they have been taught rather than think for themselves
- They might not try to think creatively
- They might fail to make connections between topics
- They often don't know how to transfer skills learned in one area to another
- They need to plan action first – and dislike spontaneity
- Often have difficulty making decisions without clear evidence

Pathological version
This would be characterized by a focus which is too narrow to function properly; by an obsessive fixation on sameness and routine.

Useful Metaphor
The autistic

Please note: I am not suggesting that people whose left hemisphere is dominant are themselves autistic, but rather I'm suggesting that the autistic mindset represents the extreme version of left brain dominance.

Now let's consider *Right Hemisphere* dominance:

Right Brain – Visual and Holistic

Likely Advantages

- Tend to be creative
- Are comfortable being flexible
- Are likely to be good at improvisation
- Are good at problem solving
- More likely to be a lateral thinker
- Have a good overview of their learning
- Often make unusual connections
- Have a good visual memory
- Often feel Inspired
- Are willing to take risks
- Are likely to be good at discussions

Likely Disadvantages

- Sometimes have an unclear concept of boundaries
- Often show poor sequential planning
- Tend to have a poor sequential memory
- Generally dislike organisation
- Sometimes have poor reading /writing skills
- Often display poor time-keeping and structure awareness
- Their progress is often inconsistent
- It is sometimes difficult to monitor how they are doing
- They are often 'late bloomers'

Pathological version
This would be characterized by a focus which is too broad to function properly; by an obsessive desire to seek out novelty.

Useful Metaphor
The psychedelic

To use a quantum physics metaphor, the *left hemisphere* prefers the particle and the *right hemisphere* prefers the wave.

If we consider the different characteristics of left brain dominance as opposed to right, then we will see that OCD is much more at home with the left than the right. It prefers the cold, logical, digital world than the warm relational, analogue one.

OCD wants its host to abandon all of the attributes of the right brain. It does not like creativity, flexibility, inspiration, lateral thinking – they are all deemed too risky. In time, OCD will cause its host to operate only from the left brain – and to a pathological degree – creating a world of ritual, protocol, procedure and predictability.

This is why it is very useful for OCD sufferers to develop their creativity – write a short story, paint a picture, craft something in wood or clay, write a poem, embroider something, design something, imagine something new, etc.

What makes us truly human is our ability to utilize both hemispheres of our brain, to draw on a rich and varied compendium of tools.

OCD wants to remove the human, to create the robot.

---

1. My views on the brain are somewhat radical and unconventional. Because of the work of Karl Pribram, I think that memories are not stored in the brain. Instead, I think that the brain is like a transducer, it can receive signals and process them. Like a TV satellite box, it allows us to access channels, but none of those channels are actually 'inside' the box. This idea is closer to something which some people call the Akashic Field.

OCD and the Twilight Zone

With each concession to it, OCD feeds itself. Every time we double check something or overdo something we are creating a world in which we mistrust our own senses. For example when I leave the house I make sure I have locked the back door and removed the key, then after doing other (sensible) checks, a thought pops into my head "Did I lock the back door?" Now, what I want you to know is that *at this point, I know I have locked the back door*, but I nevertheless feel a strong urge to double check it. If I give in to this thought, which starts to nag me, then I am undermining my own senses. *I do know that I did already check*, so I stop myself re-checking and I leave the house. The alternative would be to flirt with OCD and give it a place in my life. Once this happens, **my own senses and memories become invalidated.** I am, in effect, telling them that I no longer trust them and in so doing, I enter a kind of *Twilight zone* where reality can no longer be confirmed or verified.

The ultimate plight of an OCD sufferer whose disorder is left unchecked is to inhabit a small island of self which is disconnected from everything around them. No amount of validation can confirm what is real. Instead, doubt sits on the throne like a paranoid king, banishing peace, rest and normality.

Trusting our senses is vital, they are our main connection with the reality of this realm. Once a sailor distrusts her compass, navigation becomes impossible and they are at the mercy of the winds and waves.

This unreal world can only be tackled with a refusal to re-do that which has already been done. If necessary, make a checklist of what needs to be done (your usual OCD concerns) and as you do each, tick them off. Once there is a tick, never return or re-do. Slowly you will be returned to a world which is fresher and more real.

On the next page is a tick list – photocopy it and use it if it helps you to confirm that you have done your checks.

Since double-checking leads to a kind of unreality, we might ask the important question of why people might want to live in unreality, and the answer of course is usually that some aspect of reality have proved either unbearable or at least, difficult. Such drivers might actually form the roots of OCD.

Checking Checklist

The aim of this is to check or do something ONCE and once only. If you ignore this and return to the scene of your checking, then you are choosing to live in an unreality which will only get worse.

Use the ticks you make below to confirm your perceptions that a thing has been done (and doesn't need doing again).

To do (or check)	Tick when checked

The Future and your Powerful Imagination

OCD tends to close off a person's access to their future. Planning leads to anxiety and brings with it imagined problems and catastrophes. Everything new is seen as just another set of risks. In this way, the sufferer will come to resist novelty, surprise and the unknown. This is deeply unhealthy. If we crave only the familiar, the secure and the known, then we will atrophy our natural development, and if we wish every tomorrow to be just like today, then we are no more than a factory robot on a tedious production line.

The strongest antidote to this is through our imaginations. When we visualize and enlist all of the senses to really experience that which we are imagining, our neurons fire *as if it were real.* In this way we can reach for a future which isn't yet a reality and we can set up neural networks in that direction. You will recall that habit is overcome by habit. The negative habitual thoughts which kept you locked-in can be overcome by positive habitual thoughts which take you into a better future.

People with OCD tend to have rich imaginations, but only in service to disasters and catastrophes. These too are experienced as if they were real. Neural highways are reinforced again and again to evoke all kinds of foreboding and dread. They become the default way of thinking. These imagined dangers trigger the body just as much as if they were real. The sufferer is put on high alert, adrenaline and cortisol are released into the bloodstream, the heart pumps faster, etc. It is worth noting that these actual physical changes are being generated *purely through the imagination.*

It is time to use your powerful imagination to visualize a future that you would like rather than one which raises your stress and anxiety.

Exercise: Your Fresh Start Future

Find a comfortable place where you can relax and be undisturbed.

Close your eyes. Relax. Allow your breathing to be long and slow. Long and deep.

Now let your breathing fall into its own natural rhythm.

As you relax deeply, I want you to picture yourself in five years time. Happy and completely OCD free.

Picture yourself in a place where you'd most like to be.

Get the feeling of being completely relaxed and carefree.

In this place where you would most like to be, what can you see? Notice specific colours, textures, shapes, etc.

Your sense of smell is clearer – what fragrances do you notice?

Feel how happy you are inside. Allow those feelings to double.

See other friendly people smiling at you.

Notice how this version of you is happier. The future is bursting with happy possibilities. There is so much to explore, to do, to embrace.

Your future is within your grasp. It is all yours if you want it.

Stay with this positive feeling as long as you like.

If that exercise feels odd or takes you out of your comfort zone, just remember that it is an exercise that people with OCD do daily but with every positive reversed. Instead of a *Fresh Start Future*, they rehearse a *Stale Stuck Past*.

Mentally rehearse what you want instead of what you don't want Remember to use all of the senses where possible in your visualized future.

The Roots of OCD

OCD is about control. It manifests where people want to exert more control over their lives, their self-image and sometimes even over others. In every OCD sufferer I have ever counselled, there has been a significant event in their past where they felt tremendous anxiety *but were helpless at the time to effect change*. Usually they felt unsafe or unable to control an event, outcome or a trespass. In that heightened emotional state their unconscious decided that from then on they must *always* be in control.

In my experience, Anorexia has its roots in a similar dynamic; the assertion of control over self; a reaction to a real or perceived lack of control in other areas of life. For example, people with OCD (or eating disorders) might:

- Have been abused (sexually, physically or emotionally)
- Have had their life choices taken over by a domineering parent(s) who makes every decision for them
- Have little control over an unbearable school situation (e.g. bullying or isolation, etc.)
- Have been dominated by a friend / other person to a degree which proved frightening
- Have found themselves in a clique which they didn't like and which proved difficult to get out of
- Have witnessed traumatic situations which were beyond their control - situations which forced them to face their own helplessness

- Have been told repeatedly what to wear, think and feel by a significant other
- Have had an abusive partner
- Have grown up in a religiously oppressive environment
- Have been attacked, mugged, intimidated or raped

OCD manifests where people want to exert more control over their lives, their self-image and sometimes even over others. Control is a key driver. In this way, OCD is often an expression of self assertion in a situation which otherwise feels hopeless; an attempt to restore agency to the individual and away from the control of others.

Usually the current control is being exerted over something inconsequential, but the desire to gain control will have been triggered by something from their past which was, not only significant, but likely to have been traumatic in one way or another. So a person, who aligns their shoes repeatedly, might find the true source of their issues in the fact that they were relentlessly bullied at school.

Every OCD sufferer finds solace in their routines. If they didn't, they wouldn't follow them. That may sound harsh, but it is not a judgement, it is an insight. When we continue to subscribe to behaviours which we ourselves don't like, or which we want to stop, there is *always* a hidden benefit. If there were no pay off, we wouldn't be doing what we do. It takes a wise person to explore these underlying drivers, and when they are examined (with a good counsellor perhaps) people often find tremendous insight and cathartic release.

The *immediate* pay-off of OCD behaviour is obviously the lowering of anxiety by the prevention of a perceived catastrophe. However this is not an *underlying* driver. By *underlying driver*, I am referring to the origins of the person's need to lock down all risk and prevent harm, hurt or shame. If a person is brave enough to explore the roots of their anxieties, then tremendous healing is possible.

A skilled counsellor may help an OCD sufferer to reconnect with a buried anxiety which they had hidden from their conscious awareness for years. However we must always tread carefully when we approach traumas. Understanding why we behave as we do can be very empowering.

The following three examples illustrate the kind of things which might emerge from such explorations (it should be noted that each of these people developed OCD in later life). This is not about blame or judgement; this is about understanding and compassion.

> **Kathryn** was at a party when she was 19 and, collecting her coat from a bedroom, she was overpowered by a drunken family friend and raped. Feeling a tremendous misplaced sense of shame, she decided to tell no one. This left Kathryn with a kind of background anxiety which she carried with her, especially when she was near men. Her dark secret placed a tremendous burden on her and sabotaged many of her relationships.

> **John**'s father was alcoholic and as a small child, he saw him punch his mother in the face. He wished he was bigger and could protect his mother. On occasions his father would take all of the money from his savings bank to buy cider. It was a chaotic house to be growing up in, lacking proper structure and full of uncertainty.

> **Jenny** grew up in the house of a mother who showed her no affection. Instead, her mother seemed to see her as a kind of competitor and she would belittle Jenny in public and never praise any of her achievements. Her father was weak and did nothing to protect or comfort her - anything for a quiet life. When she was a teenager and out with her mother, Jenny would always feel anxious whenever they met anyone. There was always an underlying sense of threat as her mother seemed to delight in belittling and embarrassing her.

These examples reveal that OCD is often characterised by a need to be safe, indeed by a desire *to never be in a risky situation ever again.* But the obvious problem with that resolve is that life always carries risks, and a risk-free life is not only impossible, but wouldn't be worth living.

What has happened is that the trauma from the past has become a generalization for all future risks, great and small.

Even the tiniest of risks is seen as a potentially life-threatening trauma. In this sense the OCD sufferer's problem is not *actual* danger, but rather their *perception* of danger (which has become overblown and exaggerated out of all proportion).

Sometimes the trauma might not be from one stressful event but from a long term relationship which created fear and a sustained sense of danger. If we were just children when these things occurred for us, then their impact might be even stronger. In our early development we crave *consistency* as well as *safety*.

During therapy, it is not necessary for anyone to re-live such past traumas - in fact such a course would likely prove detrimental for an OCD sufferer. After all, *this might be the very trauma which triggered their OCD in the first place!* If the recollected 'trauma' is too painful then it may help them to describe it in the third person... so Kathryn might say *'When **she** was raped...etc.'* instead of *'When **I** was raped...etc.'* This can help provide some degree of distance on the hurt. If further distance is required, then the person might even give themselves (in discussion) no name (or a different name) when describing their trauma. So, Kathryn might say *'A long time ago, someone was raped at a party...**she**...and then **she**...etc.'* or she might use another name and say *'**Penelope** was raped once.'*

> Until you make the unconscious conscious, it will direct your life and you will call it fate.
>
> Carl Jung

> **IMPORTANT:** If you wish to do change work with a counsellor, then please choose one wisely. If possible, seek recommendations. Not all fully certified counsellors are good, just as not all fully qualified teachers are good.
>
> A piece of paper doesn't make someone good - but a proper qualification is at least a start. For me the litmus test is simple - ask yourself if you feel you are genuinely making progress and moving in the direction of a better you – healthier, happier and more hopeful.

The possibility of change and progress must always be believed. Its opposite is the surest way to remain in a 'stuck state.' Change comes when we commit to it, and when we have the tools at our disposal to make such changes. You can't steer a car which isn't moving. Making a beginning is where the change begins. Without a difference, there can be no difference.

> *If you keep on doing what you've always done, you'll keep on getting what you've always got.*
>
> NLP Presupposition

The techniques in this book ensure that you will be placing your efforts where there is most leverage. I have used them many times with many clients.

There is no substitute for supportive, one to one work with a qualified and experienced counsellor. However, if you want to make a start in the direction of understanding the origins of your OCD, then you might try the exercise on the following page.

It is possible to Identify the roots of ones own OCD by exploring the event which triggered it. Once this is understood, it is possible to see how our thoughts and feelings concerning this event may have distorted many other events which followed it.

The following exercise is designed to help you rediscover a more balanced view and clearer perceptions. Because I am inviting you to write things down, it may be best to photocopy this page or work on a separate piece of paper. Your findings might prove too private to leave in a book.

Exercise: Understanding the cause of my OCD

1. From a safe place, think back on one situation which was very stressful for you. Write down what it was.

2. Remember what you felt at the time. What emotions came with that situation?

3. Are there any thoughts or beliefs you hold now which keep you feeling these old emotions (identified in 2.)?

4. Are any recent thoughts of feelings distorted in any way? Do you exaggerate any problems (catastrophize)? Do you Jump to conclusions? Are you generalizing? Do you delete any positive aspects?

5. Challenge any distortions you have been making. If you can, restore perceptions back to a more reasonable, balanced position. Describe the difference between the distortion and the actual reality.

6. Having identified the distorted thinking, how will you choose to think differently? What thoughts and feelings would be healthier? Notice how you feel now with these new thoughts.

Using Your Hidden Code

Our minds often think in metaphor. People say things like:

- 'A weight has been lifted from my shoulders '
- 'I can see clearly now'
- 'It was electric'
- 'My stomach was jumpy'
- 'What he said really cut me to the quick'
- Etc.

What most people don't realize is that *the way we code things metaphorically affects how we feel about them.* For example when counselling people suffering from Post Traumatic Stress, they might say things like 'Every day I wake up and it's there,' and they hold their palm right up in front of their face. They are demonstrating how this past traumatic event is blocking their view of the future and they are also showing how close it is to their thoughts and feelings upon awakening. This is very useful information for the therapist. The client might also say things like 'it's as clear as when it happened.'

What has been discovered through Neuro Linguistic Programming, is that if we change the code, then the feelings will change also. In the case of the above client, it would be worth inviting them to close their eyes and access those waking up feelings when the image of their trauma is close and clear and then guiding them to see the pictures slowly receding with any sounds becoming quieter and more muffled. It would also be useful to them if the image became a little unclear, fuzzy, or blurred. As it recedes, they might notice a frame around it, that is to say, it is finite as opposed to all encompassing. The whole thing might become black and white. It might recede to the point of being just a blurry dot. Then they might imagine daubing a blob of white paint over it until there is no trace of it left. It would be good to have the client stay with its absence for a moment, and still with their eyes closed, notice how their feelings have changed. They will nearly always report an improvement.

Obviously one needs a tremendous rapport with the client to ensure they are not re-traumatised. One should first establish a safe mental space to go to (if required) and once the waking image is accessed, one should guide the client quickly towards the image receding and becoming less clear, leeching colour and focus out of the picture.

This is by no means an instant cure for Post Traumatic Stress, but it is certainly one of the tools I would use to help a client become more empowered, to regain part of their agency, to help move them away from merely being at the mercy of their memories.

Of course we should never try to deny the reality of any memories, or they will return with a vengeance; what we are doing is accepting their reality but reducing the power they have over us by altering the way we code them.

These attributes of our senses - how we see, hear and feel things - are known as submodalities (the main modalities being *Seeing*, *Hearing* and *Feeling*). We pay careful attention to *how* a person represents their experiences, *how* they remember things – these are the *sub*modalities. For example:

>They might **picture** a past event *(Visual)*
>- Near or far
>- Bright or dull
>- Colour or black and white
>- Panoramic or bound by a frame
>
>There might be **sounds** associated with this past event *(Auditory)*
>- Loud or quiet
>- Clear or muffled

- Continuous or intermittent
- To the left, right, in front, behind, below or above

They might describe a **feeling** *(Kinaesthetic)*
- Like a cold steel ball in the pit of my stomach
- Like a huge wave crashing over me
- Like a giant bearing down on me
- As a fuzzy ball of heat in my brain
- Like a coldness in my liver

You will have noticed that when we code an unpleasant experience, we can calm the feelings we have about that experience by simply *reversing the submodalities*. If it's near, we make it far, if it's loud, we make it quiet, etc.

So how does this apply to OCD? With OCD, the rituals and repeated behaviours are an attempt to quell the growing anxiety that some catastrophe is about to befall us. We feel *compelled* to follow what OCD wants us to do (which is obvious – it's a *compulsive* disorder).

It can be tremendously helpful if an OCD sufferer can describe the feeling they get when their anxiety starts to overwhelm them (at the moment when they feel compelled to act out rituals etc). Sometimes sufferers will say things like:

- It feels like a pressure building up inside of me
- It feels as if I'm very small and the world is getting bigger
- It feels like a washing machine churning in my stomach
- It feels like I'm being squeezed from outside
- Etc.

These unpleasant images and feelings can be used to the sufferer's advantage. Here's how:

Code Breaker Technique

1. Next time you feel your anxiety growing, notice how you would describe it (it might be like one of the examples above or it might be very different). Write down any metaphors which come to mind – notice how it *looks* / how it *sounds* / how it *feels*?

2. Instead of giving in to your compulsions, take a moment to be somewhere quiet.

3. Visualize the same metaphor (associated with your growing anxiety). But once you have it, quickly move to step four).

4. Taking each one in turn, reverse all of the submodalities associated with it:

   - If it is swelling, make it shrink
   - If it is a cool blue, turn it into a warm red
   - If it is near, make it far
   - If it is hot, make it cool
   - If it is huge, make it small
   - If you are small, make yourself big
   - If there is a whooshing sound, make it silent
   - If there is no sound, imagine comedy music
   - If there is a movement inwards, make it outwards
   - If something is rushing towards you, have it rush away

Just as mind and body are inextricably linked, so too are *feelings* and *code*. Change your code and you'll change your feelings.

Avoiding life itself

OCD is characterized by a perpetual state of hyperfocus. It excludes all other concerns and prevents a wider scope of attention. Specifically, it shuts out a broader range of thoughts and emotions. It disconnects the sufferer from any unwanted feelings and ultimately from interaction with others. In this way, OCD shares much with autism (the diagnosis for which seems to broaden every year). They are not similar in other respects but with both OCD and Autism, there is tremendous fear associated with abandoning a routine. Surprises and changes in plans are nearly always seen as highly stressful events – perhaps even life threatening.

Predictability is comforting to OCD sufferers, but this creates problems because everyone around them is organic and therefore unpredictable. In the OCD sufferer's mind they would like to be able to forecast everyone else's behaviour because anything unpredictable or unexpected will upset them. Surprises can be equally upsetting.

As with autism, a kind of perfectionism takes over and the OCD sufferer often creates an ideal which is forever out of reach because it never quite adheres to their standards of perfection. In this way they are frustrated and tormented by rules of their own making. There is too much adherence to rules, schedules, regulations and orders.

OCD can provide refuge from a life which has become over-complicated and challenging. Of course, OCD replaces those complications with *even more stress and difficulties.* But initially it seduces the sufferer by offering them a certain degree of comfort in the safe repetition of mindless tasks. The escape from the busy over-stimulation of life's challenges occurs entirely unconsciously and beneath the radar of the conscious mind.

If you recall, OCD much prefers the lower end of Bloom's taxonomy with its finite, safe, simple facts. It is uncomfortable with the many complexities and nuances found at the upper end of Bloom's taxonomy. It prefers repetition and routine rather than novelty and spontaneity. It wants the convergent rather than the divergent.

In this way, OCD offers a proxy life which at first appears easier than the difficulties of real life (i.e. the processes we all have to attend to). But of course, OCD is a liar and a cheat. It whispers in our ear, telling us that we don't need all of those difficult processes that we would rather avoid. It tells us that we can swap all of them for a much safer set of processes, ones we can mange easily and fixate on; bland, inane sequences of predictable routine. In this way, the organic, messy, complicated business of living is traded for the cold, dead, certainty of robotics.

> When you try to be safe, you live your life being very, very careful, and you may wind up having no life at all.
> Everything is nourishment.
> I like to say,
> "Don't be careful; you could hurt yourself."
>
> Byron Katie

OCD and Gulliver

It might be helpful to look at OCD another way and see it as a problem of 'scale.'

We can only live life meaningfully at a *human* scale. If we were far bigger than our fellows, we would be so remote that all of our previous human experience would become meaningless to us: a meal portion would be ridiculously small; we could never shake hands, we wouldn't be able to buy spectacles or shoes or clothes to fit. Indeed we would have all of the problems of the giant Gulliver (in Jonathan Swift's Gulliver's Travels). We could not live a normal life at such a large scale.

Equally, if we were somehow to shrink down to the size of an ant, then all of our previous human experience would become similarly meaningless to us; and we would experience a similar set of problems at this different scale: a meal portion would be far too much; and again, we could never shake hands, we wouldn't be able to buy spectacles or shoes or clothes to fit. We could not live a normal life at such a small scale.

Life only has meaning at a certain scale. Take a piece of sheet music, for example. If we can read music, then we can play along with the notes as they are shown on the page. If we zoom in, we reach a point where we can only see one or two notes – or maybe just the space between two notes! Now the melody is lost and there is no chance of understanding the tune. Equally, if we zoom out then we reach a point where the notes in the sheet music become indistinguishable – a cluster of beautiful notes now become just an ugly blob. Again, no music can be understood at this scale. Music, like human life, can only be expressed at the right scale

This issue of scale presents itself in the reiteration aspect of OCD, where something is repeated and the sufferer zooms in (as it where) focussing ever more closely *on a single aspect*, giving it more and more attention. When sufferers lose themselves in this feedback loop, they are living at a scale which quickly becomes meaningless. Nothing makes sense at this scale – how could it? - this is not a *human* scale.

This 'zooming-in' makes the rest of life unavailable to the OCD sufferer. They check and double check and eventually they can think of nothing else – they tumble down a rabbit hole, shut off from the rest of life.

One solution to this is that of widening perception. For example, someone checking their car is locked again and again might consider what is around the car – the street, other cars, buildings, people, etc. If these are focussed upon (and each given full attention) then the dominating OCD is softened even if only for a second. It takes practice, but it is a way out of the prison. The main thing is to contextualize what you are obsessing about and see a bigger picture. Where am I going next, now that I have locked my car? What will I be doing there? What will happen later? Whom am I likely to see? Which route will I take to walk back to my car? What will I be doing later when I return home, etc.? In this way, you are activating a 'zoom-out' to the right scale because you had 'zoomed-in' too much.

OCD sufferers stop the flow of life and in so doing they lose the meaning of the moment. It is this very hesitation and stalling which causes an over-examination of things. They zoom-in on something which they should have simply flowed past. The true value of things occurs when we flow, not when we stop and get stuck. If we re-do that which is already done, or do that which doesn't need doing, then we are developing ditches to fall into; we are stopping our journey, and it no longer flows. It is like taking the film of life and turning it into a set of meaningless stills.

Healing comes when we simply let life flow and we return to the normal speed and the right scale – a human scale.

> A centipede was happy – quite!
> Until a toad in fun
> Said, "Pray, which leg moves after which?"
> This raised her doubts to such a pitch,
> She fell exhausted in the ditch
> Not knowing how to run.
>
> Katherine Craster

What do you Really Want?

OCD is very persistent in telling you what it wants. And as we have seen it will dominate and bully you out of your own life – if you let it. Some sufferers are so busy pandering to their OCD that they have forgotten what *they* want for their own lives. Others might not have given much thought to their own goals and aspirations. It is important to consider what you want. Instead of *avoiding risk*, it is about *embracing life.*

In discussing OCD we have explored strategies to help you get *away from* OCD – and whilst that is crucial, it is also important to think about what you want to *move towards.* These can be established using a good goal setting framework.

Some folks find SMART Targeting useful. The acronym stands for Specific, Measurable, Attainable, Realistic and Timely. The idea is that for goals to be successful, we should consider whether they are Specific, Measurable etc. This is very useful, but it misses a very important component.

Sometimes the reason we don't achieve our goals is *because there is a hidden benefit to not achieving them.* There is *a pay off* for staying exactly as we are – an advantage which suits us in other ways. This is usually what stops us from moving forward – and it is the least understood part of goal setting. The following Goal Setting Tool addresses these hidden saboteurs and offers practical help on how to overcome them.

My explanation of this model is followed by some target setting forms for you to use. It is important that you fully understand the model before using the forms.

The acronym for my Target setting tool is **PAUSE** and each part is very important:

POSITIVE:

Many goals which sound positive are actually stated in the negative. Goals should be about *what you want* rather than *what you don't want.* For example, a goal of 'I'd like to give up smoking' sounds very positive, but it isn't, it's actually focusing *on what you will be losing,* not what you will be gaining. The idea of giving something up – especially something which you crave and enjoy - is not helpful to a goal. It would be better to analyse what it is you want to gain from 'giving up smoking.' It might be for example that you want better health, more money each month, cleaner smelling hair, a better atmosphere for your children to breathe, slower facial ageing, etc. Make these your goals instead of what you are losing. Focus on what you will gain. In the smoker's example, choose the benefit that would mean the most to you right now – is it health? Is it more money? Is it cleaner-smelling hair? Whichever is the most important to you right now – focus on that one and make that your goal. That way, 'giving up smoking' becomes simply part of your journey towards what you really want.

When asked what they want in life, many folks reply with a list of what they don't want (e.g. *well, I don't want to be poor*). This is equally floored. How often do you go to the supermarket with a list of things *you don't want?* Can you see how ridiculous this is? Yet many people do precisely this with their goals.

Equally, someone whose goal is 'to lose weight' is focussing on loss and what they need to get away from. A better goal might be 'to be fitter and healthier' or 'to be able to play sports with my children.' These are attractive gains which you can move towards. They focus on how you want to be. By contrast, 'to lose weight' focuses on the weight (what you don't want) and only brings you down.

Goals stated in the negative are often sneaky – and may even sound fine at first glance – after all *giving up smoking* sounds like a good goal doesn't it? *I don't want to be poor* is another. But the problem is that when we state goals in the negative, we undermine our chances of success. We are working *against ourselves* psychologically – usually without realizing it.

If you are in the habit of stating your goal in the negative, then write it down and consider what it is you want (rather than what it is you want to get away from). You can reframe your goals easily if you consider the following:

1. What do I *stand to gain* by achieving this goal?
2. What is it that I *want*?
3. Why do I *want* this goal?

Answering these questions will give you a more compelling goal and a happier journey achieving it.

So the *Positive* is all about what you want to move towards.

Here are some positive goals which an OCD sufferer *might* want to move towards:

- A more relaxed life
- To interact with others in a healthy way
- To move with the flow of life and enjoy what others enjoy
- To have a peaceful mind
- To enjoy life more fully
- To participate more fully with friends

ACTION:

If it's to be, then it's up to me. Unless *you* do something different, nothing different will happen. You are the agent of change in your life. This is about taking responsibility for making changes. It starts with you thinking about what you can do to make a positive difference.

Which changes can you make which will move you in the direction of your goals? What will you do differently?

Although this is concerned with action and doing, it is also worth contemplating if you need to make any changes to how you think about your goals. Are there any better habits of thinking that you might adopt?

One thing is certain – if you do nothing, then nothing will change. You will be no closer to your goals than before.

You need to take action.

> If what you are doing isn't working, do something else.
>
> Neuro Linguistic Programming presupposition

U**NIQUE**:

The *Action* stage should have produced some ideas and direction. It is now time to give these ideas more focus; to make them concrete. *What* changes will you make specifically? *How* will you make them? *Where* will these changes take place? Be very specific in your approach. Do you need to contact someone, prepare something, make a telephone call, buy something, get rid of something, meet someone, etc.? Think of what you need to do *specifically*. Focus in on these things. This stage is about putting the wheels in motion. It is not just about thinking, but rather about doing. It follows *Action* and it invites you to do what you need to do in a specific way. The concrete action that you take will be unique to you. You don't need anyone else or any other circumstance to hone in on the precise things that you need to do differently. This part is designed to help translate thoughts into action.

SEE:

This part is about something called mental rehearsal. When we anticipate something, we tend to make pictures in our minds of that forthcoming event. If you were going to a job interview, you would have imagined a room that the interview might take place in, you might picture a certain number of people facing you – you might picture them being friendly or stern (you might also consider what difference your 'pictures' might make to your interview's outcome). The point is, that whether your pictures are vague generalizations or very specific – you *do* make pictures in your head of imagined outcomes.

OCD sufferers are usually very good at this. *They mentally rehearse things very clearly.* The problem is that their imagined outcomes are all based on exaggerated anxieties. They picture things turning out badly, things going wrong: catastrophes which are shameful, embarrassing, disastrous or even life threatening.

This part is called *See*, because I want you to look with your mind's eye and *imagine having achieved your goal*. Take a moment to do this. What will you see? What is different? What new things are you noticing? Are there any new sounds? What are your friends (and those who love you) saying? What do you hear? What are your feelings like now that you have achieved your goal? Allow the positive feelings to well up inside of you to the point of overflowing. Let happiness percolate every cell in your body. Stay with it and enjoy it.

When people worry, they are using the skill of mental rehearsal to terrorize themselves. They are already skilled in mental rehearsal – all they need to do is rehearse what *they want* instead of what *they don't want*.

Instead of making pictures of catastrophes – and acting upon them – you CAN make pictures of happier outcomes, and act upon them. In the movies of your mind you are not just audience, you are also the projectionist.

When you mentally rehearse your *desired* outcome you are much more likely to be able to move towards it. The rehearsal helps the actual.

ECOLOGY:

We now come to what I consider to be the most important part of Goal setting. When this part is overlooked, failure is almost inevitable.

With this part, we take into consideration the whole 'eco-system' of the person. We look not just at the problem, but also at what might be maintaining the problem. In particular, we look at the *hidden benefits* of not achieving our goal. In other words, we ask the following questions:
1. What do I get from my current state?
2. Why would I *not* want to achieve my goal?
3. What will I lose when I achieve my goal?

These will all sound counter-productive; indeed you may even think they are destructive to the goal setting process. But in a moment you will appreciate the profound value of such contemplations.

I once counselled a woman suffering from agoraphobia (another anxiety induced condition). She had a profound fear of leaving the house. She had received counselling before and reached a point where she was finally able to venture outside and begin to reconnect with the world. However, this didn't last long – a week or two. Then she became agoraphobic again. She was puzzled as to why this happened and she said that now her agoraphobia was worse than ever.

The answers came when we went through the PAUSE goal setting process. All stages were useful (for example when we got to the *See* part, she thoroughly enjoyed seeing herself happy and free in her desired state – previously she was used to seeing herself trembling and fearful). The biggest leverage however came from the *Ecology* part (as it often does). When she considered what she got from her current state, she realized that when she was agoraphobic, many people would call to check if she needed anything. Many would stay for a cup of tea and a chat. There was a large social network which came to her (without her having to leave the house). When she became well, these people no longer needed to call and so many of them stopped seeing her altogether. She had lost this hidden benefit. *Being agoraphobic* meant having many friends call. By contrast, *being well* meant having hardly any friends call.

The *Ecology* part helps you to discover the *hidden benefits* of *not* achieving your goal (in this case, *friends calling*) and then try to build these benefits into your goal *in a healthy way.* In the case of the woman with agoraphobia, if she was to succeed, she needed to still have contact with many friends and *for that contact not to be based on her illness*. In practical terms this meant her asking her friends if (once she felt well) they would meet her at a café, in the park, at the shops – and even drop by her house now and then – not as a help, but as a friend for a chat. Once this network was established, she lost her agoraphobia. She remains free of it to this day. I would suggest that her agoraphobia no longer had a function. It no longer served a purpose.

Another example of hidden benefits preventing a person from achieving their goal comes from someone who told me decades ago that they had a great idea for a novel. They described it as a sure fire bet for a best seller. They didn't disclose the idea, but they got a lot of pleasure out of telling others how amazing the book would be. Of course, all these years later there is still no sign of the book. Not one page has been written. So what is going on? What is the hidden benefit to the person never writing that book. It's simple. If the book is ever written, then people will judge for themselves if it's great or not. It might be a complete flop. *But if it never gets written, then it can always be claimed as a great book – even though it doesn't exist.*

To assist someone in this situation, it would be useful to help them to see this hidden benefit, and to help them to focus on making the book great, rather than fearing the rejection of others.

Driving around a roundabout may keep all of your options open, but if none of those options are taken, then, in effect you have no options. People in 'stuck states' often remain on a roundabout believing it makes them more free.

Looking honestly at what you get out of your current behaviour requires a degree of maturity, honesty and self-reflection. We often pretend to ourselves that there is no pay-off, that there are no hidden benefits to us staying as we are (not achieving our goals) but there nearly always are.

When we understand what those benefits are, we can set about seeing if we can get them in healthier ways whilst still moving towards our goals. For example if a smoker wanted to become a non-smoker and have cleaner healthier lungs, they might find that they miss the camaraderie of smokers together chatting at break time. If this benefit is lost, then the person is likely to start smoking again. A more ecological approach would involve protecting this benefit by making sure that they still enjoyed the camaraderie and social interaction with their colleagues (they might stand with them at break times without smoking or they might find other ways to interact with everyone).

When a hidden benefit is not considered, you will find that it is not ignored so easily. It will behave like a spoilt child and will sabotage all your attempts towards your goal. It usually acts in unconscious ways and often the person will be at a loss as to why they keep failing to reach their goal. With PAUSE we deliberately bring the hidden benefits into conscious awareness so that they can be looked after.

A person wanting to be healthier, who currently snacks in the evening, would be wise to consider *what they get from snacking*. Maybe they feel *comforted*? Maybe they feel *loved*? Maybe it makes them feel *rewarded*? Maybe it is a moment just for ourselves in an otherwise busy day where others are the focus? The secret is to find ways to feel comforted, loved and rewarded by other means – healthier means.

> Your visions will become clear only when
> you can look into your own heart.
> Who looks outside, dreams;
> who looks inside, awakes.
>
> Carl Jung

Work out some of your goals now using the PAUSE process (there are blank forms on the following pages):

PAUSE Goal Setting Form

POSITIVE: *Write your Goal. Make sure it is stated in the positive. It should be something you want to move towards, not away from:*

ACTION: *What will you do? What changes will you make? What will you do differently? What will you start?*

UNIQUE: *What will you do specifically? What do you need to do in practical terms? Focus on the detail. Make it happen. Make necessary arrangements*

SEE: *What will you see, hear and feel when you achieve this goal? Put yourself in the future. Enjoy it fully. Experience it as if it had already happened. Note what will be different.*

ECOLOGY: *Honestly examine the hidden benefits of not achieving your goal. Find healthier ways to get these same benefits.*

PAUSE Goal Setting Form

POSITIVE: *Write your Goal. Make sure it is stated in the positive. It should be something you want to move towards, not away from:*

ACTION: *What will you do? What changes will you make? What will you do differently? What will you start?*

UNIQUE: *What will you do specifically? What do you need to do in practical terms? Focus on the detail. Make it happen. Make necessary arrangements*

SEE: *What will you see, hear and feel when you achieve this goal? Put yourself in the future. Enjoy it fully. Experience it as if it had already happened. Note what will be different.*

ECOLOGY: *Honestly examine the hidden benefits of not achieving your goal. Find healthier ways to get these same benefits.*

PAUSE Goal Setting Form

POSITIVE: *Write your Goal. Make sure it is stated in the positive. It should be something you want to move towards, not away from:*

ACTION: *What will you do? What changes will you make? What will you do differently? What will you start?*

UNIQUE: *What will you do specifically? What do you need to do in practical terms? Focus on the detail. Make it happen. Make necessary arrangements*

SEE: *What will you see, hear and feel when you achieve this goal? Put yourself in the future. Enjoy it fully. Experience it as if it had already happened. Note what will be different.*

ECOLOGY: *Honestly examine the hidden benefits of not achieving your goal. Find healthier ways to get these same benefits.*

PAUSE Goal Setting Form

POSITIVE: *Write your Goal. Make sure it is stated in the positive. It should be something you want to move towards, not away from:*

ACTION: *What will you do? What changes will you make? What will you do differently? What will you start?*

UNIQUE: *What will you do specifically? What do you need to do in practical terms? Focus on the detail. Make it happen. Make necessary arrangements*

SEE: *What will you see, hear and feel when you achieve this goal? Put yourself in the future. Enjoy it fully. Experience it as if it had already happened. Note what will be different.*

ECOLOGY: *Honestly examine the hidden benefits of not achieving your goal. Find healthier ways to get these same benefits.*

Recovery Summary

I hope this book has helped you to understand OCD more thoroughly. Knowing how OCD works is vital for recovery. Its mechanisms are devious and its parasitic nature is insidious. But this book also offers practical exercises and strategies, each of which could make a huge difference. Taken collectively they comprise a formidable opponent to OCD.

Please remember that OCD will put up a fight. It will resist eviction. But every sufferer has the power to get rid of this unwanted guest once and for all.

You will make the most progress if you:

1) Understand your OCD fully; where it comes from, how it works, what feeds it, what starves it, etc.
2) Learn the many techniques in this book.
3) Practice the techniques and make them your new habits.
4) Stay with it. You will only be defeated if you give up. Habit is overcome by habit, but it takes time to establish new habits.
5) Reflect honestly - 'What did I do today which made things worse?' and 'How will I do things better next time?'
6) Ask yourself, 'What did I do today to make my situation better?' and 'How can I build on this?'
7) Take time out each day to relax very deeply. Mind and body go together. Relaxing the body will help relax the mind.

The path of progress is not a straight line; it is wiggly containing setbacks as well as victories. The main thing is that when you step back and review your progress you will find that even a wiggly line has an overall trend, and you will not be where you once were. That is why it is important to take heart and carry on. Always.

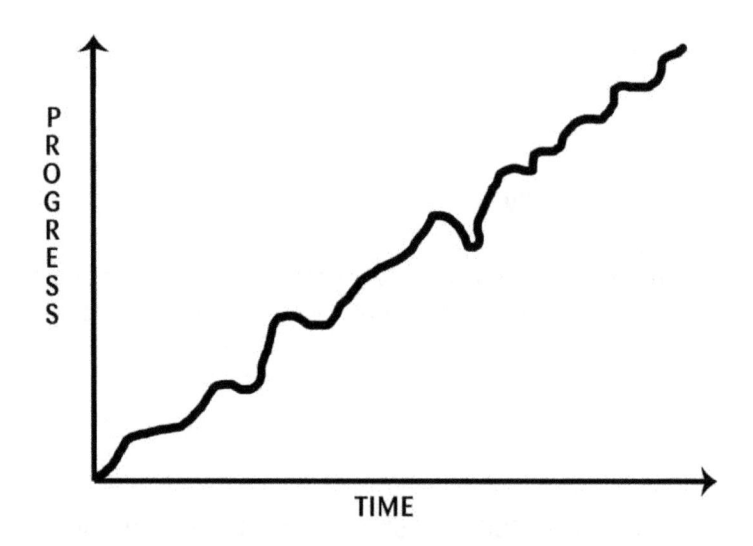

Progress vs Time graph showing a wiggly upward-trending line.

If you have suffered with OCD for any length of time, then your commitment to your progress could be life-changing and incredibly liberating. Here are a few thoughts to help you stay the course:

Instead of:	Try thinking
This new way feels weird	New habits always feel weird at first
I've made a mistake again	I can learn from each mistake
I can't be bothered	I'll try some different strategies
This is way too hard	New habits take time
I felt more comfortable with my OCD	OCD was ruining my life
I give up	I'm only defeated when I give up
It didn't work	It may work next time
I can't do it	I'm going to train my brain to do it
I'm hopeless	I'm brave and I can do this

Key Points Summary

This summary is intended to offer a reminder of the many insights, principles, strategies and techniques in this book. It is not a substitute for the content it refers to. It is merely a reminder:

OCD is a serious matter; it is not just an interest in safety or cleanliness.

OCD is like an unwanted guest. If you defend it, it takes over.

The amount of time given to OCD by a sufferer is shocking.

The core of OCD is always logical (e.g. safety of self or others).

If you feed it, it doesn't go away. It grows.

If you can understand it, you will be better equipped to deal with it.

OCD links thoughts to actions as if every thought must have happened.

OCD is an unreliable witness. In fact, it's a liar.

OCD compels you to perform ritual behaviour on a promise that your anxiety will drop once you've done it. But after the compulsion, anxiety levels remain high. OCD is a cheat.

OCD is a bully.

The real choice is whether you choose to feed or starve your OCD.

OCD displaces the amount of space you have for your real life.

Over-doing is as bad (or worse) than not doing.

Resisting OCD only makes it persist. Pushing it away only connects you to it more.

Thought displacement is a great way to overcome an OCD compulsion.

An Amazonian tree frog can defeat an African elephant.

Whatever you give your attention to will become more real for you.

New habits will feel uncomfortable *at first*.

Your Success takes practice.

Habit is overcome by habit.

Your efforts will produce the greatest gains at the precise moment when you feel compelled to engage in a ritual. That is the Critical Moment.

You have to leave your comfort zone if you want to eventually be more comfortable.

OCD makes people misinterpret information and catastrophize.

OCD puts you in a state of fight or flight. It tells you there are serious threats when there simply aren't.

OCD is like a mind-parasite. It makes the host behave according to *its* needs.

Playful surreal thoughts help to weaken the link between our thoughts and what is actual. We can have lots of thoughts which don't become reality.

People with OCD have very active imaginations – they *imagine* all sorts of disasters.

OCD sufferers can take charge of their imaginations – to imagine so many things going right for them.

Neurons which fire together wire together.

When we change our thoughts, we change our brain pathways.

Make sure friends and family don't like you having your OCD (especially if it makes you the underdog or them feel superior).

OCD keeps people stuck on the Knowledge level of Bloom's Taxonomy – the first basic rung – and prevents more meaningful cogitation.

Practice being playful because OCD insists you must be responsible at all times.

Use intensive thinking as a thought displacer. Remember the examples of a deckchair and a potato.

You can't argue someone out of OCD. All evidence will only be used to support the need for OCD.

OCD wants you to live in a 'left brain' way. The extreme version of this is like a kind of autism.

OCD prefers you to disconnect from all human feelings (except fear). There is a flattening of affect.

It is good to practice/appreciate 'right brain' skills – creativity, drawing, painting, poetry, prose, dance, drama, music, play, etc.

OCD seduces the sufferer into an unreal world –
a Twilight Zone where their own senses are not trusted.

OCD often comes from earlier events where the sufferer felt
helpless and extremely anxious.

How we code our experience can give us a clue as to
how we can defeat rising anxiety.

Using the Code Breaker Technique,
we simply reverse the submodalities.

OCD can become one big doctor's note,
excusing us from life itself.

OCD occurs when we slow the film of life down to static images,
when we stop the meaningful flow.

OCD makes us zoom in too close
until life itself cannot be understood.

When you zoom in too much, deliberately zoom out –
contextualize and see a bigger picture.

Because OCD keeps insisting on what it wants,
it is very important to commit to your own goals.

The PAUSE goal setting tool is very useful.

Be careful to note any hidden benefits you get from your OCD –
this is the Ecology part.

Recovery is possible. You have the resources.

The path of genuine progress contains setbacks
as well as victories.
It is a wiggly line rather than a straight one.

Further information

I'd love to hear what you thought of this book. I do hope you have found it helpful. You might like to:

Email me: enquiries@positive-effect.co.uk

Visit my web site: www.positive-effect.co.uk

Leave me an Amazon review: Search for *'Unlocking OCD'* and *'Nick Buchanan'* then write your review.

About the Author

Nick Buchanan continues to work as an *Integrative Counsellor* using a wide variety of helpful modalities; and as a *Clinical Hypnotherapist* using trance states to help clients deal with a broad range of issues and concerns. Clients can decide if they would like counselling, hypnotherapy or a mixture of both. Nick meets with clients either in person or via video link (Skype, Zoom or similar). In this way, his clients can be from anywhere in the world.

His aim is to help people to discover their own inner resources to the point where they go beyond just coping and start to live life full measure.

Nick is a member of the **National Council of Psychotherapists** whose aim is to uphold the highest standards within the various therapeutic fields.

In addition to writing about anxiety disorders, Nick has written two

500 page guides to Shakespeare plays: **What Happens in Shakespeare's King Lear** (ISBN 978-1-291-63507-2), and **What Happens in Shakespeare's Macbeth** (ISBN 978-1-326-55213-8). Both are available globally.

In relation to his Shakespeare guides, Nick was interviewed twice for local television. Once on *Arts Alive*, and once on *About Books* (both *BAY TV* productions). The interviews can be found on YouTube.

Nick also writes children's short stories; one of which, *'The Worm, the Telly and the Nightingale'* was short-listed for the Cheshire Prize for Literature. It was published in *Word Weaving* which collected together the prize shortlist. It can be found here: https://bit.ly/3dUwlTQ

For his book ventures, Nick uses the website: **www.nickbuchanan.co.uk**

Nick is in demand as a Staff Development Trainer and Keynote speaker. He covers a broad range of subjects: *Creativity in the Classroom, Developing a Work Family, Thinking Skills for Innovation and Problem Solving, Assertiveness for Healthy Relationships, Spiral Dynamics and the Evolution of the Self, NLP as a tool for Personal Development, Excellence in Customer Service, Leadership and Management, Team Building, etc.* See: **www.positive-effect.co.uk**

Nick has an interest in the ideas and work of Philip K. Dick and (since #23) is the designer, layout artist and occasional writer for the free online magazine *PKD Otaku*, which explores the writings of Philip K. Dick. All contributors give their time and skills freely. Copies of the magazine can be downloaded here for free: https://philipdick.com/resources/journals/pkd-otaku/

Nick has also worked as an Illustrator producing a wide variety of pieces in Designers Gouache paint and pencil:

His illustration and design clients include Radio Times, Hambro Guardian, Arrow Books, Aladdin Books, Best Magazine, Nursing Times, Balance Magazine, Yorkshire TV, Lloyds Bank, etc.

Nick was a Lecturer in higher and further education for over 25 years teaching Graphic Design, Illustration, Thinking Skills and teaching the teachers on the Cert.Ed. course.

He grew up in Liverpool when summers were long and children played in the street. As a teenager he delivered papers, stacked shelves in the Co-op, was a bicycle delivery boy and worked for a commercial photographer as a studio-hand and as a developer of colour films and prints.

He believes that schools have very little to do with education and are more concerned with institutionalization. However, he is grateful to inspirational Teachers like Richard Newington and Mr. Wynn Williams, who made a difference.

Nick is a passionate reader enjoying a wide variety of authors, including; Alan Garner, Alan Moore, Alfred Bestall, Anthony Burgess, Anthony Peake, Arthur Koestler, Arthur Miller, C. S. Lewis, Charles Bukowski, Clifford D. Simak, Colin Wilson, Cormac McCarthy, David

Mercer, Dennis Potter, Doris Lessing, Dr. Seuss, E. F. Schummacher, Edna O'Brien, Edward DeBono, Erich Fromm, Edgar Allan Poe, Franz Kafka, George Orwell, Gerard Manley Hopkins, Harlan Ellison, Harold Pinter, Herman Hesse, James Joyce, John Steinbeck, Jonathan Miller, Jorge Luis Borges, Ken Wilber, Lewis Carroll, Loren D. Estleman, Michel Faber, Milan Kundera, Neil Kramer, Oliver Sacks, Oscar Wilde, Peter Shaffer, Philip K. Dick, Philip Larkin, Philip Pullman, Ray Bradbury, Richard Brautigan, Roald Dahl, Robert Sheckley, Roland Barthes, Russell Hoban, Seamus Heaney, Seán Street, Stephen King, Susan Hill, Ted Hughes, Theodore Sturgeon, Umberto Eco, Walter Mosley, William Blake, William Golding, and William Hjortsberg, William Shakespeare.

Nick Buchanan
Dip (Integrative Counselling – Level 5) (UKAIT)
Certificate (Counselling Supervision) (UKAIT)
Dip (Clinical Hypnotherapy) (UKAIT)
NLP Master Practitioner (INLPTA)
NLP Trainer (UKAIT)
BA(Hons). Graphic Design (LJM)
Cert.Ed. (University of Manchester)
Community Life Coaching (Metanoeo / Association for Coaching)

www.positive-effect.co.uk　　email: enquiries@positive-effect.co.uk
www.nickbuchanan.co.uk　　email: hello@nickbuchanan.co.uk

Acknowledgements

The following people have helped directly or indirectly with the writing of this book. I am grateful to them all.

Paul Henderson, Stephen A. Hopley, Colin Power, Wendy Burton, Richard Grannon, Mike Millar, Nate Nicholson, Neil Kramer, R.D.Laing, Sarah Hanlon, Edward DeBono, Roger Van Oech, E.F.Schummacher, Arthur Koestler, Erich Fromm, James L. Adams, Milton Erickson, Virginia Satir, Fritz Perls.

You cannot find peace by avoiding life.

Virginia Woolf